Liberation:

A Quest For A New Humanism

Liberation:
A Quest For A New Humanism

AN AFRICAN STORY OF REVOLUTION, EXILE AND HOPE.

A SEEKER'S QUEST FOR FREEDOM, JUSTICE AND PEACE

HASHIM EL-TINAY

To order additional copies of this book, contact:
Xlibris
1-888-795-4274
www.Xlibris.com
Orders@Xlibris.com
719729

Contents

Dedication

To my sister, soulmate & pioneer Afro-Arab journalist leading the way for women dignity in Africa and the Middle East, Sayda Mariam Mustafa Omer El-Tinay and hopes for a liberation that can set us free to work together for the realization of our shared dreams for social and economic justice, peace and dignity for all people and a New Humanism in the 21st century.

Foreword

I feel sincerely privileged to have the rare opportunity of sharing my salient and pertinent thoughts on the author's valiant attempt to contribute to contemporary intellectual literature on current trends in social justice and governance.

The stark truth is that the world is in desperately traumatic flux, with humongous challenges facing the global community on all fronts. That is the absolutely cogent reason why the author's evident leaning towards an advocacy for freedom, social and economic justice, peace, equality, unity and human dignity, as made manifest with this brilliant book, can only be commended.

I have for long held the view that mankind's most distressing dilemma is that most people remain irrevocably shackled down by norms, nuances and beliefs that are at best antiquated, and at worst, totally out of sync with present global realities.

That is probably why the two words "liberation" and "revolution," have, over the past two centuries, grown into integral components of the total human experience, with no contemporary historical text being ever complete without the insinuation, in whatever relevant context, of the two words into the fabric of the narrative.

However, one thing is clear. The massive manifestations in mass protests, violent tendencies and social dislocations which these two words have come to represent are clear indications of the abysmal inadequacies of ruling classes to respond appropriately to contemporary challenges, simple and complex, in different parts of the world.

Additionally, the disenchantment of the marginalized segment of the world's population with the seemingly obnoxious status quo is becoming increasingly evident even in the world's supposedly most sophisticated democracy, America, where, only recently, a prominent Presidential candidate, seemingly and totally out of the blue, suggested a social democratic revolution as panacea to the evolving ills that are becoming a recurring decimal in the American society. It is instructive to note that the author himself has subscribed to this particular view since his days as a young legal scholar in his native Sudan.

Unfortunately, it was this very perception, and its attendant view of how society could be re-structured for justice and equality, that inexorably led to the author's flight into self-exile from Sudan in 1975. Today, the world is perhaps fortunate that he can contribute to such profound intellectual discourse as a result of his citizenship of an egalitarian society that is totally representative of the best in freedom of speech and thought that the free world has on offer.

The author's journey is quaint testimony to his own leaning towards the quest for peace, social justice and economic parity. He has had a brilliant career on the local and international diplomatic turf, and could have quite easily perched on the wings of executive and diplomatic influence in Khartoum, Washington and New York, to feather his own nest, and join the club of the nouveau rich.

Rather, believing totally in the theories that he promotes and pontificates on, he chose to walk away from all the seeming glitter, and tread his own path of ideological self-belief, much to the chagrin of his friends and associates.

I feel particularly privileged that, in reading this book, as I am sure many others will agree, one is exposed to the author's noble quest for truth, equality, peace and social and economic justice. I have no doubt whatsoever that many people will be grateful to the author for sharing tidbits from his journey from a place of intellectual suppression and tyranny to one of a quest for global enlightenment, human dignity, social justice and peace.

Conclusively, it is my sincere and fervent hope that, just as I have, you will find this journey into the past, and the resultant excursion into the present, as inspiring and illuminating as it has been for me.

I commend this exquisite piece of intellectual work to you, dear reader, and also encourage you to give your unalloyed support to the author as he strives to propel his efforts for the emergence of a global culture of peace to the next pedestal.

HRH Yomi Garnett, MD
Royal Biographical Institute
Philadelphia, Pennsylvania.

Acknowledgments

This book would not have been possible without the understanding and solidarity of so many people and especially of the French and American people who enabled me to find refuge and since 1985 settle in the West.

First thanks to France that accorded me the political refugee status in 1985 and for America's embrace when it accorded me the privilege of becoming an American citizen in 2002.

This book would not have been possible without the love and the extraordinary solidarity of my Sudanese wife Mona Mohamed Sanusi Omer El-TINAY, my French and American wives Anne Lise Kraft and Shari Lynn Curtis and their families and their communities in Sudan, Europe and the United States.

This book would not have been possible without the welcome I have been enjoying since 2009 at my Saint Mary's Court at Washington DC's historic Foggy Bottom-George Washington University Campus-Friends Communities.

This book would not have been possible without the embrace of the research, academic, media, think tank, diplomatic, buisness, political and the global virtual communities of LinkedIn, FaceBook, Twitter, Pinterest, Instagram.

I am grateful to my good friends professors Jean & Michelle Sellier, Bechir Ben Yahmed founder of Jeune Afrique, and le Père Michel Lelong of France. John Farina of George Mason University,

Soulayman Nyang of Howard University, Onley Cahill, of Palm Beach, Florida, Mamadi Diane, president of Amex International, Reginald McFail, businessman and Howard Ross founder of Cookross, Barack Obama and Bernie Sanders in the United States. Dr. Mansour Khalid, ex Minister of Foreign Affairs, Dr. Sidiga Washi, Dr. Aicha Kayal, Educators, Imad Ali, Development Banker, and Dr. Hassan Ismail Obeid, Sociologist, in Sudan.

Two people that I had the pleasure and privilege of becoming friends with who deserve a special recognition and gratitude and who shared my passion to advocate for a better world, are Yuji Yokoyama, Japanese journalist and African-American journalist Jerome James, my Linkedin friend whose interest, encouragement and many phone interviews were crucial to my writing this book.

This book would not have been possible without the love and the extraordinary affection of my parents, all my brothers, sisters, uncles, aunts and village, town and city communities in Kordofan, Omdurman and Khartoum in my country of origin, the Sudan.

Finally, this book would not have been possible without the love, extraordinary affection, unity of mind, heart and spirit between my sister, soulmate and journalist Sayda Maryam Mustafa Omer El-Tinay and myself since our childhood.

What unite us is a deeper awareness and a consciousness that opened our eyes thanks to early conversations we started to have on the beauty as well as the mammoth challenges facing our cultures and societies of origin in Africa, the Middle East and the global community.

What continues to unite us is a sustained conversation, an awakening to our purpose in life to continue being authentic and passionate advocates for freedom, social and economic justice, peace, equality, unity and human dignity.

Preface

"The one thing that is stronger than all the armies
in the world, is an idea whose time has come."

-Victor Hugo

It was a wonderful feeling to visit the Louis Armstrong original home
in New Orleans, Louisiana in the Southern United States in the year
2000. In all moments of learning and discovery his amazing and
inspiring song "What a beautiful world!" comes to mind. So life is a
great gift that deserves to be lived, happily, fully and meaningfully.
However, the 24/7 news cycle these days keeps throwing at us a
stream of ugliness and violence-driven news that make the world
seem to be a fundamentally chaotic, messy, dangerous and ugly place.
As Mark Siljander clearly explains in his book "A Deadly
Misunderstanding": a Quest to bridge the Muslim-Christian
Divide, the root cause of our misery is our failure to admit that we
all seem to be hostage to ideologies rooted in erroneous, ossified,
mutually exclusive and, in contrast to our technological innovation
breakthroughs, out of date, obsolete and debunked paradigms
and in the lagging behind social sciences, rife with and hostage to
conflicting, limited, self-righteous, narcissistic, arrogant and bellicose
narratives. The more we think about this, the more we are inclined

to wonder about the challenges as well as the opportunities of this the 21st Century.

The pessimists would tell you that the ongoing ideological polarization and the hazards of a globalization rigged in favor of Wall Street, widening the gap between the rich 10% and the poor 90% continue to feed the deadly misunderstanding. This situation seems to be driving us straight into an inevitable apocalypse and a tragic end of the world. The optimists would, on the other hand, tell you that we now have an opportunity to stop, think out of the box, evaluate, practice humility, self-criticism and seek the truth. That it is time for a thoughtful revisiting of the history of our human journey, evaluate them and use the lessons learnt to attain a deeper human consciousness, harbinger for a much-needed human awakening that can unleash our better angels, a prerequisite for the liberation of the human spirit and the emergence of a more just 21st century humanism so that we can all share in the enjoyment of the gift of life and the pursuit of our happiness.

This, I believe, has been the root cause of all revolutionary movements in human history and the source of inspiration of liberation struggles at all times. We all know about Nazism, Fascism, and the excesses of the unbridled extremisms of Marxism and unruly Capitalism. Many people continue to suffer the effects of exploitation by colonialism, imperialism and apartheid, in Africa, Asia and Latin America and the tragic and inhumane slave trade, the Holocaust, the ongoing Palestinian-Israeli fratricidal killing, the Arab Spring, the balance of nuclear power terror, religious fundamentalism, terrorism and the emergence of many grassroots movements trying to channel the mounting popular anger and rage against the establishments and the bureaucracies, which are supposedly managing our societies around the globe speaks volumes to the failure of most elitist systems of governance, at local, regional, and global levels, to cope with the world's contemporary and increasingly complex challenges. The social media revolution and the democratization of information fed the growing thirst, hunger and yearning of all people for freedom, dignity, social and economic justice and peace.

The 99% ninety nine percent poor and disenfranchised are sick and tired of an economic system that favors and caters only for the rich 10% one percent. The dysfunction of the American Congress, supposedly the apex of democracy, and the publicly stated policy of the American Right to make President Obama a one-term president, naturally provoked a pushback from the Left. Hence, Bernie Sanders' audacious and, I would add, right diagnosis of the American political, economic, and social predicament. That's why he proposed a Social Democratic Revolution, as a remedy to America's ills of poverty, income inequality, corruption, racism, militarism, greed, fear, violence and dumb wars. As I mention in this book, I have believed in this vision since my law student days in the University of Khartoum and continue, more or less, to believe in it today.

Like many before me and many after me, if people continue to refuse to be the change they need to see in the world, and do nothing, I was forced into exile from the motherland and fatherland I love, the Sudan since 1975. My crime was thinking out of the box. Thinking differently. Refusing to go with the flow of the mainstream groupthink of hypocrisy and towing the line of whoever was in power. I was imprisoned and persecuted simply because of expressing my point of view. Politically, I have always thought that between the two dominant ideological extremes of extreme Marxism and its dictatorship of the proletariat and the extreme Capitalism that imposes the dictatorship of the 10% rich over the 90% poor, a Social Democratic hybrid governance model would be preferable to guarantee a much-needed social and economic justice.

I feel blessed to have, after a forty years journey of diplomacy, exile, advocacy for societal transformation through peace and social and economic justice in Africa, the Middle East, and Europe, and finally in America, I have now finally found in the United States of America, a country that guarantees my basic freedoms, of thought, expression and action, in its Declaration of Independence, its Constitution and in its Bill of Rights. I feel blessed to be embraced by my new Washington, DC, community of Foggy Bottom, and George Washington University neighborhood in Northwest Washington, D.C. close to Georgetown.

Indeed God works in mysterious ways. I remember that I had a great feeling of joy after my successful experience at the WUS General Assembly in Tokyo, Japan in 1962. In my flight out of Tokyo international airport heading to Hong Kong, I wrote on my diary that I love learning and teaching so much that I pray and hope that God help me have a life of service of the common good rooted in research, knowledge, education, communication, teaching and advocacy. Today, 54 years later, I am an American citizen, a freelance communications and language professional, and a peace advocate, living on the George Washington University (GWU) campus, named after George Washington, the founding father and first president of the United States of America. I am also a GWU visiting scholar, a member of the grassroots FRIENDS organization and was president elect of the Saint Mary's Court residents association in 2014, on Washington's historical Foggy Bottom neighborhood which was a black neighborhood.

At the intellectual and the ideological level, and thanks to my grassroots political involvement with the Democratic Party as a founding member of its grassroots arm Organizing for Action (OFA) which twice helped the historic election of Barack Obama to the presidency, I was recognized by the President and First lady Michelle Obama for my humble contributions to the cause. I continued speaking up via my monthly peace Quest Forum at Saint Mary's Court and made my voice heard through the social media.

https://youtu.be/KnGPwPbnvxo

As a result I was elected as president of the Saint Mary's Court resident association in June 2014 and was appointed an honorary member of president Obama's Kitchen Cabinet in 2013. Like all of us who believed in Obama's promise and who genuinely hoped and worked for real change, I was disappointed by the angry push back of the American right and the declaration of Mitch McConnell, the Republican leader of the Senate, when he declared war against Obama and the popular vote of the American people that carried him to the White House when he said: "We will make President Obama a one term president". The American people wanted better and knew better. The world needs progressive ideas and progressive public policy to move forward. So they told Mitch who is boss in a democracy and reelected Obama in 2012 to the chagrin of the right wing forces of reaction.

If the American people and American democracy made history by the election of Barack Obama as an antidote to the Bush presidency in 2008, Bernie Sanders rise to lead a social democratic revolution in America was the expression of an America that decided to make history again by leading in the realm of ideas. By articulating candidly and forthrightly his vision for the transformation of America, Bernie Sanders' courageous and authentic critique of the corruption and dysfunction of the existing system accurately expressed the popular sentiment around the country and indeed around the world. It also resonated with the majority of the people who feel that the political elites have become too powerful, selfish, cynical, corrupt and oblivious to their suffering.

This might be an opportunity to clarify what many of my acquaintances, claiming to be my friends, consider as an enigma about my socio-professional life. Many of my contemporaries and colleagues in my professional journey as a diplomat, a United Nation's staff, a researcher, a seeker, kept scratching their heads about why I was never satisfied with all those dream jobs that I was so lucky to have! Why I always refused to join the club of the "rich and famous", which they were aspiring to join! My answer is that, as a thinker I was never fooled by the superfluous and the glitter of any job. I always tried to ask the fundamental question: in this job, am I making a difference in the life of ordinary people or am I serving those who are exploiting them?

Because, in essence, I have never bought into the dominant paradigm and the unjust and rigged system it created everywhere. My moral compass and my guiding star helped me distinguish between truth and fiction. Intuitively I was never at peace with injustice in any way shape or form. Intuitively I my heart yearned for a better tomorrow of justice, by serving the noble promise of societal transformation and the dawn of a new humanism for the 21st century. As someone who has never forgotten the call of the famous African Marxist thinker and leader of Guinea Bissau, Amilcar Cabral, who challenged the African intellectuals to commit class suicide if they really wanted to serve the African people. No wonder then that I chose to part ways with a job as a Sudanese diplomat, a UNESCO staff, a World Bank, (now a few blocks from where I live and work staff), being a part of the %10 ten percent, to be a part of the 90%, it was no surprise that Sanders' vision was music to my ears as I have been fighting for this same vision my entire life.

From a spiritual and intellectual perspective, I smiled when I heard Bernie's inspiring mainstreaming of America's need for a Social Democratic Revolution. As someone who is a victim of persecution because of having dared to embrace such a vision since 1963, it felt like the heavens were talking to me and telling me that I am finally home.

I am eternally grateful to my family and so many friends and supporters and all of the support that I have received from so many people who believed in the justice of our common quest for truth, equality, peace and social and economic justice. Because of their good will, their faith, their, moral and material support, and thanks to my life in Washington, in the District of Columbia, America's beautiful capital city today, which became my home away from home, I am happy to be able to share with you, dear readers, snippets of my long and ongoing journey away from tyranny and toward freedom and my/our quest for a more enlightened humanity, social and economic justice, dignity and peace.

Many years ago Alexis de Tocqueville warned in *"Democracy in America* (appearing in two volumes: 1835 and 1840), that modern democracy may be adept at inventing new forms of tyranny, because radical equality could lead to the materialism of an expanding bourgeoisie and to the selfishness of individualism and as Bernie Sanders would add oligarchy. In such conditions we lose interest in the future of our descendants...and meekly allow ourselves to be led in ignorance by a despotic force all the more powerful because it does not resemble one.[17] Tocqueville worried that if <u>despotism</u> were to take root in a modern democracy, it would be a much more dangerous version than the oppression under the Roman emperors or tyrants of the past who could only exert a pernicious influence on a small group of people at a time.[3]

In contrast, a despotism under a democracy could see "a multitude of men", uniformly alike, equal, "constantly circling for petty pleasures", unaware of fellow citizens, and subject to the will of a powerful state which exerted an "immense protective power".[3] Tocqueville compared a potentially despotic democratic government to a protective parent who wants to keep its citizens (children) as "perpetual children", and which doesn't break men's wills but rather guides it, and presides over people in the same way as a shepherd looking after a "flock of timid animals".[3]

Source: <u>https://en.wikipedia.org/wiki/Alexis_de_Tocqueville#On_democracy_and_new_forms_of_tyranny</u>

Indeed in "the beginning was the word" and Bernie Sanders, I would add. Like him and the millions he inspired in America and, thanks to the social media, in the world, I believe that time is dangerously running out for a more peaceful America and a more peaceful world. Both deserve and desperately need a peace-centered vision. It is time for contemporary thinkers, philosophers and social scientists, to think out of the box, be imaginative and innovative enough and have the wild ambition to create heaven on earth rather than continuing the suicidal path of racism, militarism, greed that is leading us all toward what could be hell right here on earth!.

It is precisely to do something about this, that I decided to liberate myself from the slavery of a rigged, corrupt and tyrannical system, sacrifice my personal survival, think out of the box, and dare, despite the obvious odds, to dream a bigger dream for all of us, articulate that into a vision and a mission that I have been sharing since 1985 through my two grass roots charities: Salam Sudan Foundation (SSF) and the International Peace Quest Institutes' (IPQI) intercultural, interreligious and interethnic peace vision, and roadmap with the world.

I spoke at various conferences, to various media, and presented papers at forums from Indonesia's Jakarta to America's Los Angeles, from Holland's the Hague to Lebanon's Beirut, from Sudan's Khartoum to France's Paris, from Nigeria's Ibadan to Rwanda's Kigali, from America's Washington to Korea's Seoul and in many Washington DC universities, such as George Washington University (GWU), Howard University, Georgetown University, American University, George Mason University and various think tanks, churches, synagogues, Mosques and colleges.

WHY I AM WRITING THIS BOOK?

I am writing this book to share my experiences, my failures, successes, and the lessons I learnt along the way as a witness and as an advocate. I do hope that this story and journey, both rooted in a striving for a much-needed revolution of liberation from bondage, can inspire others to dare thinking out of the box and dream the bigger dreams. The trials and tribulations of my revolt and exile did not shake my hope and my quest for freedom, justice and peace. I hope to give the reader, a taste of finally hearing a voice of the excluded and the voiceless. I also hope that this story is representative of the millions of our human stories here in America, in Africa, in Sudan, in the Middle East and indeed in the whole world. Stories that the corrupt, rigged and cynical political systems, their establishments and their gatekeepers everywhere and especially in the corporate media do not want you to hear.

The world is clearly undergoing a governance crisis. People's yearnings are greater than the governance systems can deliver. The

Sudanese people, the American people and indeed all people feel that they deserve better. All the people deserve to realize their big dreams of a so far illusive liberation revolution. My hope is that a day will come when the dawn of a new humanism will break. For this to happen everyone of us has a personal responsibility to do his/her part. That starts by seeking knowledge and wisdom, wherever one can find it because it is our gateway to a deeper understanding of our humanity's journey. This I believe is unattainable without 21st century governance systems that are based on guaranteeing the fundamental human rights expressed eloquently in the preamble to United States Declaration of Independence, 1776 which states:

(We hold these truths to be self-evident, that all men are created equal, that they are endowed, by their Creator, with certain unalienable Rights, that among these are Life, Liberty, and the pursuit of Happiness.

That to secure these rights, Governments are instituted among Men, deriving their just powers from the consent of the governed, That whenever any Form of Government becomes destructive of these ends, it is the Right of the People to alter or abolish it, and to institute new Government, laying its foundation on such principles, and organizing its powers in such form, as to them shall seem most likely to effect their Safety and Happiness.

Prudence, indeed, will dictate that Governments long established should not be changed for light and transient causes; and accordingly all experience hath shown, that mankind are more disposed to suffer, while evils are sufferable, than to right themselves by abolishing the forms to which they are accustomed. But when a long train of abuses and usurpations, pursuing invariably the same Object, evinces a design to reduce them under absolute Despotism, it is their right, it is their duty, to throw off such Government, and to provide new Guards for their future security).

The world will be a happier place if we all can work hard to liberate ourselves from the three evils of racism, militarism and greed. In so doing, all people would be capable to realize their yearnings and aspirations for human dignity, through freedom, democracy, social and economic justice, peace and prosperity. This is my Sudanese-American dream.

I hope you find it both enjoyable and inspiring. Through my early involvement as a student in two partially successful peaceful revolutionary experiences at the University of Khartoum and then at the University of the Sorbonne in Paris, and as Bernie Sanders keeps telling all who care to listen, I have always believed that when millions of people embrace a vision whose time has come, organize and stand up demanding its implementation by providing their energy, skills, money and all they have got, there is nothing that they can't do.

I hope you do too. If you do, please go to my website at: <u>www.hashimeltinay.com</u> and donate to help us have the resources to take our work for the emergence of a culture of peace to the next level. We are better together.

Now to "Liberation: Exile Notes". I hope you enjoy it.

Introduction

"The purpose of a writer is to keep civilization
from destroying itself."
Albert Camu

Historical Overview and Context
Ancient African Nile Valley Roots
Sudan's Kingdoms of Antiquity

The Washington, DC, Sudanese embassy website makes the following
pitch about Sudanese history that I find to be a great segway to what
I want to share with the reader and illuminates the purpose and the
essence of my journey and why I am writing this book.

Africa's Nile Valley:
A Melting Pot of Ancient cultures
The Cradle of Humanity and a Humanist
Civilization

All this is part of an indigenous development which was
intertwined with Egyptian institutions without losing its original
vitality. Eventually, many of the indigenous elements, which derive
from African origins, outlived the Egyptian infrastructure and
reappeared, more or less unchanged, at later periods in Sudan's

history. Furthermore, as if to reinforce the distance between the Kushan realm and Egypt, the downfall of the Kushan kingdom came about not from the north, but from the south, from Africa's Ethiopia, another neighbor which has traditionally played an important role in Sudanese history. In around 330 AD, the downfall of the Kush civilization occurred at the hands of King Ezana of Aksum, whose invading armies Ethiopianized the country; a language ancestral to present day Nubian was first introduced, and pottery styles became distinctly more African than Mediterranean. The Kushan period is instructive, if only because it serves as a reminder to those whose own cultural and historical perspectives have remained trammeled along racial or religious lines, that the Sudan as a country is capable of generating its own specific characteristics, acquired from both the north and the south, and analysis furthered by reference to subsequent periods in Sudanese history."

Author's Note:

"Those who make peaceful revolution impossible
will make violent revolution inevitable",
John F. Kennedy

Most of us who are familiar with the ancient history of Kush, Nubia and the Nile Valley civilization would have no problem with the facts in this introduction. However, because all Sudan watchers, and especially since this regime's treacherous and diabolical military-Islamist coup d'etat of June 30th, 1989 in Sudan, we and the whole wide world have become aware of the regime's strategy of lies, denial, deception and disingenuous manipulations and diversionary tactics. They became the hallmark of its tyrannical and cynical machinations. This is how they are cherry picking such pieces of historical information to claim a false connection to an old glory, hiding behind a smoke screen of ancient history to divert attention from their present day atrocities, violations of human rights and horrendous crimes against humanity and a tragic presence that they created by practicing racism, militarism and greed all, alas, in the name of a religion of freedom, unity and peace, that they hijacked in the dark of night on June 30th, 1989. So let me say that this is neither smart nor funny. How do you compare your present abysmal record of hijacking a peaceful people and a potentially great country and religion through lies and the cruel practice of tyrannical and wanton violence? Kush's ancient kings you are citing here must be turning in their graves because of the genocidal inhumanity that characterize your miserable and failed "Islamist" experiment.

In public, the whole wide world knows that the relations between the powers that be in both the United States of America and the Sudan have been bad since the Islamist military coup d'etat of June 30th, 1989 and their takeover of power in Khartoum. In private we do not know what is really going on.

So this introduction appears to be another smoke screen and a diversionary tactic to dupe the public and fake Sudan's tragic and sad present day realities. Politics aside, and based on mere facts the peaceful people of the Sudan have been victim and hostage to a cruel, corrupt, cynical and tyrannical dictatorship composed of of the so called "Muslim Brothers", who are a fringe minority of callous and greedy politicians who succeeded in hijacking the Sudanese Army and the Sudanese state and kept the country and its people hostage for the last 27 years, and worst, in the name of Islam. So this embassy website historical overview and introduction, although academically acceptable, is a clear denial of the ongoing tragedies imposed on the Sudanese people, their neighbors, Africa, the Middle East, the larger world and, especially on all Muslims, hypnotised by corrupt and rigged governance systems of tyranny, misinformation, propaganda, conspiracy theories, ignorance of the world and myopic emotionalism.

I do hope that this story and journey, both rooted in a striving for a much-needed revolution, exile and hope and my quest for freedom, justice and peace can give you, dear reader, a taste of finally hearing a voice of the voiceless. I also hope that this story is representative of million stories in Sudan, Africa, the Middle East and the world, that the corrupt, rigged and cynical political systems and their corporate media gatekeepers do not want you to hear.

All people, including the American and the Sudanese people, deserve better. They will sooner or later realize their big dream of a so far elusive liberation revolution. The day will come when they realize their yearnings and aspirations for the emergence of free, democratic, united, peaceful and prosperous societies, that they can all be proud of.

Chapter One

AFRICA: GENESIS

HUMBLE BEGINNINGS: AFRO-ARAB ROOTS

FROM SUDAN TO THE WORLD

AFRICA, EUROPE, ASIA, AND AMERICA
A PEACE QUEST JOURNEY OF A GLOBAL CITIZEN

"Time heals griefs and quarrels, for we change and
are no longer the same persons.
Neither the offender nor the offended are any more
themselves".
Blaise Pascal

If man is a product of his environment, then the story of my life
is a reflection of the love and healthy environment of my happy
childhood. My family's emphasis on education and the values they
and my mentors instilled in me contributed to a stable upbringing.
Their support and encouragement laid a solid foundation for me to
spread my wings and take to the sky; it was the launch pad of my life's
journey and my quest to discover the world. Those early years opened

my eyes to the challenges and the opportunities that life brings on a daily basis.

> "We made from water every living thing.
> Will they not then believe?"
> (Surat Al-Anbiyaa – The Prophets: 30, Quran)

The black clay lands of North Eastern Kordofan and the golden sands of the Sahara Desert surround the town. This region is well endowed with wild Acacia (Hashab) trees that bear abundant amounts of gum arabic and immense areas of fertile land that allow for the farming of a variety of crops, such as millet, corn, tomatoes, cucumbers, oranges, melons, etc. The town itself is beautiful, with perfectly symmetrical avenues lined with Neem trees and large spaces for recreation and sports. Two-thirds of the population is composed of the Muslim, Arabic-speaking Jomaa, Bazaar, Habbaniya, and Bidairiya tribes, while the remainder of the population is comprised of the dynamic and hardworking Fellata people. After decades of Anglo-Egyptian rule, Sudan achieved its independence from the British in 1956.

I arrived in the world on December 23, 1939 in Umm Ruwaba, Sudan, four months after the beginning of World War II. My home town Umm Ruwaba is a strategically located town situated between El-Obeid, capital of Kordofan state, and Kosti, a port city linking the North and South of the Sudan on the White Nile that also links Sudan's capital Khartoum with Kordofan's capital city El-Obeid Railway line.

Community Events

Within my family and community, there were many festive events. The three major events that were celebrated were based on the Islamic calendar. First, Al Mawlid (Arabic for birth), which was a one-week birth anniversary and celebration of Prophet Muhammad's life and works. The celebration took place at a big square a few blocks from our home, where there were tents overflowing with members of various Sufi bands, who were carrying their drums, dressed in colorful garb and chanting the praises of the Prophet. There were also rows of kiosks displaying an array of yummy sweets artfully sculpted in the shapes of various animals, as well as small cafeterias and restaurants, which offered people sandwiches, beverages and seats to rest on after walking around. Second, was the Eid El-Fitr, which was the end to the fasting of Ramadan, one of the five pillars of Islam. The community gathered together to enjoy food, sweets and drinks, share stories, and to celebrate the end of the month long fast. Third, was the Sacrifice, which celebrated the story of Abraham and his faith in God. The celebration included a community prayer, a slaughtering of a lamb and a large BBQ, where people visited with one another.

Now that this is out of the way, here is what I want to say. Enjoy.

SUDAN

1 - 1

REVOLUTION: MYTH AND REALITY

"Those who make peaceful revolution impossible,
will make violent revolution inevitable." John F. Kennedy

The security officer at the Johannesburg Jan Smuts international airport told me that my name was in South Africa's black list and that I was not welcome in South Africa after looking at my Sudanese passport. He informed me that they have a hotel in the airport grounds where I can spend the night. That I have to take the first flight out of the country. This was the first time for me to come face to face with the White South African Apartheid system that I was, like many others, working hard to undermine. From my perspective I was doing the right thing. The world would be better off if we could get rid of systems that are rooted in the three evils of racism, militarism and greed. Apartheid South Africa had the arrogance and the shameless and false claim that it represented the front line of the defense of White Christian civilization. My University Education, which is a major investment in any young man or woman, was how I had this adventure. At the hotel bar, I met an American International Herald Tribune reporter who was also unwelcome. We exchanged views and information and parted ways. In the morning I flew to Gaborone, in neighboring Botswana, called my friends in South Africa to come join me at my hotel which they did. That was how my mission was accomplished despite the scorn and machinations of an inhumane, immoral and corrupt system. It was my education, awareness and my determination to act on my beliefs that led me on that path. This is why I believe that education can be the best window to an individual's self and life discovery.

The British initially founded the Gordon Memorial College, named after the notorious General Charles Gordon who was known for his role in taming the revolting Sudanese natives and dervishes in the 1800s, as an institution to teach the Sudanese the skills necessary to participate in the administration of the country.. My father attended this college back in the late 1920s, which led him to his career as a government official. The name was changed in 1956 to the University of Khartoum after Sudan gained its independence from England.

The University of Khartoum is strategically located on a very lush and exclusive neighborhood on the Western bank of the Blue Nile, that was reserved for the residencies of high-ranking government officials. An important bridge linked the capital, Khartoum, with the neighboring city of Khartoum (Bahri) North. The main building of the university, which were constructed with red bricks and consisted of two floors, was the central library. Every other building was placed around the library, which included the lecture halls, staff offices, laboratories, conference halls, dorms, school buildings, soccer fields, the university administration building and other facilities. The campus itself was very green, with lush grass filling open spaces, flowers decorations and rows of trees lining the walkways.

Like most students at the time who did well in high school, I aspired to become a medical doctor by attending the School of Medicine. However, reading Dr. Kwame Nkrumah's autobiography and my awareness about issues of injustice in my family, in Umm Ruwaba and the larger community, inspired me to help people by working for ore justice and hence considering the study of law. My grades would have enabled me to join either school. I needed to consult and do my search on the subject. Luckily my cousin, Mohammed Ibrahim El-Imam, was a bright star in the Khartoum University Medical School. This was a good reason to pay him a visit and seek his counsel. I asked him if I could study medicine and at the same time play soccer, which was my favorite sport. He said "no way". So I asked him about an alternative. He proposed law school as their workload was lighter than that of medical school. He added anecdotally that another aspect that was worth my consideration is that medical students envied law students their ability to reconcile hanging out in the cafeteria with their female colleagues and do well academically more so than medical students could. That is how I decided to join the law school at the University of Khartoum.

I spent five years in the Faculty of Law. We studied both British common law and Islamic Sharia law. The British common law included torts, sale of goods, public, international and criminal law. British professors taught the subjects. The Sharia law included contracts, marriage/ private relations, inheritance, bequests, wills etc. The faculty of law consisted of lecture halls and a good library. I had the opportunity to serve as a member of the Law Student Association. I realized that Mohammed was right because the workload was not as heavy as it would be in medical school.

The University of Khartoum's social and cultural environment in the early 1960s was as enriching and vibrant as the academic one. In addition to advocacy and cultural activities, the campus provided a fertile ground for free expression. The military dictatorship censored the press within the country, which suppressed political views; however, the student newspapers, which were written and pasted on the walls of the student cafeteria, were not censored and allowed for free expression of ideas.

The University of Khartoum's campus in the early 1960s was also a haven for all sorts of Western youth, mostly Europeans and Americans, who wanted to venture into Africa. Since they were mostly adventures yearning for the joy of travel and the pleasure of exploration, these longhaired visiting students and other youths traveled mostly on low budgets. They mostly communicated in the English language, which removed the language barrier and allowed them to easily make friends with the University of Khartoum students. Given the value of hospitality in Sudanese culture (Afro-Arab) to the foreigner, many of the visiting students ended up sharing dorm rooms and meals with university students. The students were able to share ideas, have fun and arrive at some kind of understanding and solidarity as young people.

1 - 2

THE SUDANESE REVOLUTION:
WAITING FOR GUDU
THE POLITICIANS AGAINST THE PEOPLE

Genesis of a Peaceful Social and Economic Justice Revolution:
Students, Politics and a Deferred
Big Dream for Sudanese Societal Transformation
October 21, 1964

"Common sense is in spite of, not the result of education".
-Victor Hugo

Sudan got its independence as a country in January 1956 after years of Egyptian British condominium rule (1898-1956). A parliament was elected in anticipation of the change. It was composed mainly of Afro-Arab tribes from the northern part of the country. Over the course of the next two years the independent government did not do well. There were socioeconomic, cultural and political problems. The first coup d'etat of November 1958, gave Sudan its first military government. At first, the military were reluctant to take over the country. When Prime Minister Abdalla Khalil felt he was going to lose in an election, which meant he would lose his power, he persuaded the head of the military to take over the government. That is how Chief of Staff Major General Ibrahim Abboud overthrew the elected parliamentary government in a bloodless coup d'état.

This was a very unfortunate precedent in the ongoing Sudanese governance saga. It planted the first ominous seed of racism, militarism, greed, intolerance and mistrust that set the Sudan in the wrong direction, which continues until today. Trashing the Constitution and opportunistically manipulating the army, which was supposed to be the guarantor of the unity of the nation, under any pretext, was and remains a heinous crime and an act of treason. Prime Minister Abdalla Khalil was a conspirator who took an approach that was culturally alien and mediocre, which replaced the power of votes with the power of guns and bullets. His actions made a lot of people weary of politics and politicians. The incredibly cynical and vicious political elites were perceived as diabolical, self-centered, arrogant and selfish. They didn't give a damn about fairness and peaceful exchange of power through the ballot box.

People in South Sudan were especially suspicious of most of the Sudanese northern politicians. The first Sudanese governments after independence were dominated by Northern Sudanese, who were perceived by the Southern Sudanese as being different due to their Arab and Muslim culture. Historically, the northern regions of the Sudan were Arabic and the southern regions were made up of indigenous Africans. The people in the South knew that the Northern Arab Sudanese were favored by the outgoing British administration in terms of who would run the country once they left. Under British colonial rule, the North Sudanese benefited from education and training to man the different development projects, notably the world-famous and largest cotton farm in Al-Jazeera. Because of all this, the people in the South were very wary of the people in the North. As the British were leaving, the people in the South thought that the Northerners would become the new colonizers. In 1952, Southerners revolted against the military, which caused an anti-northern kind of movement in the South. This was the genesis of a North-South dilemma, which impacted the country throughout its turbulent beginnings.

Students, being a part of the younger generation, were naturally more idealistic and motivated by an innocent yearning to be instruments for change and service for the common good of society.

My earlier experiences in WUS that I explain in another chapter in this book, helped me develop a deeper awareness and nourished my initial interest and love of community service in my university, my country, the region and the world. The opportunities and investment the organization made in me at age 23, played a key role in opening my eyes to the challenges and the opportunities for students to become involved in community work and develop a taste for serving the common good. These insights naturally led to my involvement in student politics.

The Khartoum University Students Union (KUSU), our student government, was trying to change the situation in the country. There were three ideological groups in the student body: the Democratic Front, the Islamic Front and the Social Democrats.

The Social Democrats were my group. I became their representative and was elected Vice President of the whole student government.

5.16.2004

Hashim El-Tinay, Vice President,
Khartoum University Students Union (KUSU), 1963-1964

The military government wanted to solve the problem of the
South with the power of arms and KUSU was against that. We all
thought the situation should be resolved politically. KUSU knew
the governance within Sudan needed to change. We considered
the different ideologies from all three groups within the student
government. We asked ourselves; why should we be consumers of alien
ideas and ideologies (the Muslim Brotherhood and the Marxists)?
Why can't we create our own brand? We were trying to offer a new
path that was a creative synthesis of ideas taken from all ideologies,
something that is reflective of Sudanese authentic nature, culture
and spirit.

In early 1964, KUSU took an initiative to be the voice of the
people. Through a memorandum, KUSU presented a united position
that the military government of General Ibrahim Aboud resign, so
that the people could elect a new government. KUSU's ten member
executive committee delivered the memorandum to the office of the
President. Instead of adhering to the memorandum, the government
arrested the ten members and sent them to Kober Prison. KUSU's
governing council, consisting of 40 members that represented
different political parties on campus, held an emergency meeting
and elected a new executive committee to replace the one that was

in prison. They created a mandate to carry on the unfinished work of bringing an end to the military dictatorship and paving the way for democracy.

KUSU created forums that addressed the issue of how to manage the country's problems and challenges in a civilized way: through political conversations and. We thought the problems of the country should be solved through discussion and arrive at a consensus that all sides of the political spectrum could agree upon, and not with the guns. The respect of the rule of law could help us on the path to democracy and freedom. Different parties presented their points of view on how they saw the crisis and what solutions needed to be considered. Our discussions were very respectful, peaceful and straightforward; it was almost academic. There wasn't any fighting, just simple discussion. It was the beginning of a resolution and it felt good to do the right thing for our country. Our role as student leaders was to give a voice to the people. We had the space and we had the power to do so. We were just providing a service to the larger community and the nation. We all believed the country would be better off to find reasonable solutions. Sometimes common sense doesn't always prevail, though.

The fact that KUSU was meeting at all was very big at the time, because no one had a right to speak about politics by order of the military dictatorship. As part of our tradition of practicing student democratic governance, we decided to continue organizing forums to debate the issues of the country. At the time, the university was an island of knowledge and a laboratory of ideas. Being the main university in the country at the time, freedom of thought was very much respected and protected. There were a series of these forums in October of 1964, which culminated into the October 21, 1964 event that saw the intervention of the police and the shooting of students.

On Wednesday October 21, 1964, KUSU organized a forum under the title "The Resolution of the Problem of the South Resides in the Resolution of the Problem of the North". This event was special because we invited thinkers and politicians from outside the university community to come and address the theme of the forum, which made the government nervous. The event started at 6pm in the University Barracks on the western part of the Blue Nile. Up until this last forum, neither the military nor the police were involved in any of our activities. We were peaceful students trying to do our part by participating in politics. However, when we invited

all the political people from both the North and South in to discuss
these issues, the military got nervous. The military thought that
KUSU was joining forces with the opponents of the government in
the discussion. Then it became dangerous. The government sent the
police to the university to disrupt what we were doing. The police
sprayed tear gas to frighten people and cause them to disperse. We
told the students to protect themselves, take cover, not to use force
and avoid the police. Of course, some of the students reacted with
stones and whatever they had to defend themselves. In these kinds
of situations it's difficult to have a handle on everything. It was very
quick. A brief intervention of gunfire and then the police left. Ahmad
Al-Qurashi was the only one to get killed, that night, and Babikir
Abdel Hafeez was injured and died a few days later. We attended to
those who were hurt, caring for some on campus and taking others
to the hospital. I don't think the military realized it at the time, but
the fact that they did what they did was considered as crossing a line
in terms of the public opinion. Why send police with guns inside the
university, which is supposed to be an oasis of freedom, and shoot
students? Those shots created a buzz in the community and a big
moment. It was the catalyst of a movement that marked major change
in our country.

Immediately after the shooting, I walked to Al Souk Al Arabi
(the Arabic Market) in search of black cloth. My fellow students and
I were in mourning for the loss of two of our students. In hindsight,
I remember being calm, almost remarkably so. I suppose it was faith
and culture, or both. I think most people in Africa are like that.
Basically my attitude was one of someone who feels the weight of
responsibility and is laser focused to do his part. This feeling might
be from my family's DNA, since I was the grandson of a chief on my
mother's side and a grandson of a judge and businessman on my
father's side. But the reality was that I was simply a law student who
had been elected Vice President of KUSU and was thrust into a time
of crisis. Whatever the reasons, I was very calm when I had no right
to be. I was focused on managing what was happening around me in
the best manner I could. While looking for the cloth an idea came
to me. I decided to include red, green, white and black cloth in my
search, which were the colors of the national flag of Sudan. The
government officials chose these colors because they were symbolic
of the ethnic, cultural and religious diversity of the country. It was an
attempt at unity in a country that was anything but unified. The idea
was to wrap our martyr's body in the national flag to symbolize that

he died for the country's cause. It would be an ironically unifying symbol. The cloth wasn't part of an overall planned strategy. We lost this young man and it had to be highlighted. He had made a great investment in our struggle for freedom, unity and liberation from the tyranny of the military. In Khartoum Hospital, we took turns guarding the body in the basement. We were careful not to allow the military to come steal the body so we wouldn't have anything to rally around. All night we organized with trade union and political leaders for a big mass demonstration the following morning. It was in the hospital's basement that, in my capacity of Vice President of KUSU, I met many leaders, including Sadig El-Mahdi, one of Sudan's ex Prime Ministers.

More than 90,000 people representing students, teachers, workers, farmers, lawyers, judges, and diverse Sudanese associations and trade unions, showed up early morning to walk with us from the hospital to Abd Al-Mun'im Square near Khartoum Two to protest the military violation of the independence of the university and the usage of gunfire that killed our martyrs Ahmad Al-Qurashi and Babikir Abdel Hafeez. People showed up in droves. We had many speakers who took turns in condemning the military government and reiterating the need for a return to democracy. Among those was a professor at the University of Khartoum, named Dr. Hassan El-Turabi, who later became the ideologue for the Sudanese Islamists. It was very clear that we the people were out there to express outrage against the tyranny that killed our brothers. For the most part, we were still using peaceful means just showing up and speaking up. There were calls for bringing down the government. In a big mass of people there is a feeling of empowerment and feeling of vindication of the cause. There's also a collective courage. There were some people who got a little too excited. They torched some police cars when they came around. Despite that, we managed to end the day without additional bloodshed.

In the days after the demonstration, KUSU came together with leaders from the various Sudanese Trade Unions and Professionals, which included farmers, professors, workers, doctors, etc. We formed the National Profession Front (NPF), where we regrouped and decided on how the strategy and the tactics that could lead to victory. My classmate, El-Shaikh Rahamtalla and I were chosen to represent the students in the NPF. We wrote press releases and informational materials to be distributed in the neighborhoods and participated in other daily activities. One of the more important decisions was that we chose to use the university's conference room as the headquarters of the NPF and the revolution. The university was still considered an oasis of sorts by the rest of the country. Even though the police had come there once, they did not come back. Things started to fall into place, almost like an alignment of the stars. All the differences between Africans and Arabs, Christians and Muslims were fanned by politicians, who usually thrive on the divisiveness of people to preserve their interests in power and wealth. People are people and generally, and if left alone, can work things out and hopefully get along. So, the NPF became the official voice of our nation. We started discussing how to dislodge the government. We formulated the tactics and planned the demonstrations, but also prepared for the worse. We went over all the scenarios that were possible. Then came the day when we surrounded the palace and asked the government to depart.

A part of our plan focused on having a demonstration at the iconic Khartoum presidential palace, a few blocks from the university campus on the West Bank of the Blue Nile. We wanted to make it clear to the military rulers that they had to go by being faithful to the memorandum submitted to them earlier by our imprisoned colleagues. Once we finished deciding our course, I was asked to pass on this directive to the people waiting at the student-staff cafeteria where the majority of our participants were waiting. Our decision was to move in mass to encircle the palace. We would walk from the university to the palace chanting. Our slogan was, "To the palace until victory," which in Arabic is "Illa El
Kasr Hatta El Nasr." Our plan and goal was to stay outside the palace and pressure the dictatorship until we achieved victory.

In hindsight that was probably the first moment when I felt that we were making history. We were writing a chapter of dignity. It was an incredible feeling of responsibility because of the dangers that could ensue from all of this. There was a lot of faith. There was no fear. There was a total belief in the justice of the cause. Whatever sacrifice it took, it was meant to be. That was the price to be paid for our dignity. We moved ahead immediately. The people assembled knew what to do without me saying another word. The palace was seven blocks away, a straight shot down University Street.

The weather was pleasant, which made it perfect for going to a demonstration. I got a ride with medical professor Dr. Salah Abdel Rahman Ali Taha to the demonstration in advance. When we arrived at the big square outside the palace, we saw the military with big machine guns. We had to tell the people not to be violent, to say what they needed to say without confrontation. Still there was some shooting and someone was shot in the stomach very close to where we were. We took the shooting victim, put him in the car and drove to the Khartoum Hospital emergency room. These are things that stay with you. I was just doing the right thing, nothing more than that. This was what I was supposed to do, this was the right thing to do, and the rest I leave to God.

It took about 10 days before we heard the official government announcement that they would agree to our terms: to organize free and fair elections for a transitional government, which included some members of the NPF, led by Sir El-Khatim El-Khalifa, an educator, as Prime Minister.

The National Professional Front (NPF) appointed a new government. During that time, there were many more meetings we entered into with the political parties jockeying for power. The Left, the Right, Muslims, Communists and all in between participated. It took a lot of meetings in different venues to hash out an agreement on the transitional government and who would oversee the elections. Since there were now politicians among our group, it started to get a little more contentious, but it was still subdued. People were still in a mood to do the right thing and had not yet adopted a self-centered posture.

Watch the below link of Aljazeara documentary on the Sudanese October 21st, 1964 successful and peaceful revolution.

https://www.youtube.com/watch?v=HvpehzUOpsQ

Even today, every year, the 21st October 1964 Revolution is celebrated and continues to inspires people in the Sudan and beyond. This historic event, that took place 47 years before the Arab Spring, inspired poets, writers, journalists, singers, musicians, and artists of all persuasions to express themselves. Some of the most mobilizing and amazingly profound and beautiful songs were inspired by that popular revolutionary movement and moment in Sudan's modern history. However, in the often unethical and at times "dirty game" of politics, it is said, that history is, alas, written by the "victors". Both the Left, represented by the Communists, and the Right, represented by the Islamists, were trying to take credit for the victory excluding the participation of others. They tried to exclude KUSU's student parties, such as KUSU's Social Democrats, Africanists, Arab Socialists etc... as well as the role played by all other political parties in the revolution.

Through these actions Sudan's Islamists succeeded in imposing a narrative that anointed their thinker, Dr. Hassan El-Turabi, who spoke at the first KUSU-organized rally, as the sole voice of the revolution and connived to hijack the Sudan in the name of a racist, militarist and greed driven political project that imposed tyranny, misery and fear on a peaceful people and divided the country. Sudan's Islamists have since June 30th, 1998 succeeded in taking the Sudan hostage through their infamous June 30th coup d'etat against a democratically elected government. Sudan's "Islamists" succeeded in hijacking the Sudanese people's' unfulfilled dream that was unleashed by the short-lived victory of the popular and peaceful October 21st 1964 "Revolution" over a military dictatorship. They outsmarted everybody stole the country's army, tanks and guns, all, alas, in the name of Islam. In so doing, they succeeded to keep our people hostage for the last 27 years, by successfully tricking and duping all the Sudanese people, the region and the world.

1 - 3

SUDAN:
HOW REVOLUTIONARY DREAMS
TURNED NIGHTMARES AND
PERMANENT COUP D'ETATS?!

THE KHARTOUM APRIL 6TH, 1985 INTIFADA

Just like what we did back on October 21, 1964 the Sudanese people rose up against the Numeiry's dictatorship and the Sudanese army sided with them putting an end to the country's second dictatorship. I spoke about this and my return to the country and my running for a parliament seat in the 1986 elections elsewhere in this book.

DEMISE OF SUDAN'S
SECOND MILITARY DICTATORSHIP
May 25th,1969 - April 6th 1985

Between 1983 and 1985, I continued my professional and research activities in Paris, France while keeping an eye on developments in the Sudan. I became an outspoken advocate for the overthrow of Sudan's second military dictatorship of Gaafar Numeiri in the same way we have done with the country's first military dictatorship under General Ibrahim Abboud during our October 21st, 1964 Khartoum University students' uprising.

Like we did in October 1964, the Sudanese people decided in April 1985 that they had enough of tyranny. So they poured into the streets demanding political change. Unfortunately, the only organized group that could intervene to fill the vacuum was the same military. That is how General Abdel Rahman Swar al-Dahab took over in a bloodless coup d'état. The coup climaxed after days of Sudanese public protests. Gaafar Numeiri was coming back home from a visit to the United States, where he had gone to have an annual physical examination and to ask President Ronald Reagan for more economic aid. During that time, and for Cold War calculations, the US saw the Sudan as an important ally since it supported their Middle Eastern policy. Even though the coup might have been a source of concern for the US, since it was one military leader taking over from another, it didn't cause a ripple.

We, in Paris, were glad to get the news and I explained to the Parisian public via media commentary what was going on in the country. led a delegation of Sudanese democratic activists who represented Salam Sudan on a trip to Khartoum to meet with the new interim President. It included Dr. Hussein Nabri, a French trained Sudanese economist, and Hassan Nabri, a Sudanese businessman. In a meeting with the new president at the iconic Republican Palace on the West bank of the Blue Nile, we advised him to stick to his promise to hand over power to an elected government in the span of a year, as the people started to lose faith in the military.

While I was in Sudan, some of my friends and relatives from my hometown, Umm Ruwaba in Kordofan, approached me about working with them on their political convention. Their district had just been given a new seat in the Parliament. They figured since I understood government and diplomacy that I would be an asset to them. They also reasoned that since I had experienced firsthand the oppression of the previous government that it would be good to see the country's resurgence up close. Eventually, that turned into persuading me to run for the seat. My friends were members of the Umma Party, led by Imam Sadiq El Mahdi.

> However, I had and still continue to have serious reservations about the political culture which I thought was the root cause of our predicament. However, as a democracy and a human rights advocate I felt the opportunity was timely for me to return to the country and work for a democratic Sudan that can accommodate all of its citizens. As politics is the art of the possible, I knew that I had to compromise with the politicians to be able to fit in, since I was an outsider. I however was in it for service not for power or wealth. So I told my people that I had two conditions to accept running:
>
> 1) that they unite behind my candidacy, and
> 2) that they get the blessing of the Umma Party's president and Imam of the Ansar El-Mahdi religious group.

They agreed on both, and I was invited by Sadig El-Mahdi for breakfast in his residence at Omdurman on the western bank of the Blue Nile. He was running a slate of candidates so it made sense to let him give his approval to my candidacy. Although there was something not quite right about the chemistry, he agreed that I should be on his ticket. El Mahdi promised that he would support me with funding and transportation. The meeting went about as well as could be expected, but I still walked away with a feeling I couldn't quite put my finger on.

El Mahdi did not like the fact that I was an outsider that had been forced upon him. In the end, I waited for funds and transportation that never materialized. Instead, El Mahdi supported another candidate, which caused the party to split their votes. I ended up funding most of my campaign out of pocket, which led to some financial hardship. I eventually had to sell a piece of property to pay my debts and I was defeated in the election. Welcome to the world of politics!

THE POLITICAL CULTURE UP CLOSE:

BETWEEN NOBLE CALLING AND DIRTY GAMES?!
MY FIRST SUDANESE POLITICAL CAMPAIGN 1986:

"When People fear the Government There is Tyranny,
When the Government Fear the People There is Liberty"
Thomas Jefferson

Despite all that I had to endure, running for a seat in what we hoped could be a democratic parliament was one of the best experiences of my life. I still believe I was there at the right time, in the right place and with the right message. There were some very touching moments. I remember six and seven-year-old kids at school in the morning dressed in white chanting, "There is no light without El-Tinay." My campaign symbol was a lantern. My message centered on lighting the way. Interestingly, the symbolism of my campaign meshed with my family's creative side, since I had an uncle who was famous for his poetry.

Many of the older women came out to speak about my dad and mom, since they were well known in my region. We had music from the best Sudanese singers. The campaign rallies were in the countryside, so it was quite interesting. I had fun. Deep in my heart I felt I was following the right path. I was not really focused on getting a job or getting power. The issue for me was now I had an opportunity to make my voice heard. So long as people are there to listen I want to share with them what I know. I totally discounted the politics. It became about awareness. I used the pulpit to discreetly warn the people about small politics. This is my position until today. Many politicians hate people like me because I am not talking about anything they love, which is power and money. I'm interested in helping people see the light. I want to make politicians accountable and keep them real. I'm focused on what people can be. I dislike the lies that are told to gain and hold power. I always fear that the real voices, the voice of the people, will never be heard. My run revealed to them the contradictions professional politicians have between rhetoric, action and the objective limitations of the traditional party system.

The Khartoum Al-Siyassa Newspaper editor asked me to write an article about my election experience and my disappointment in the political elites that was published on the 21st of October 1986, which said in part, "as the road to Sudanese democracy is still long and full of landmines I was returning to my exile in Paris and continuing my professional and political work. But en route to Paris I was asked by my sister Sayda El-Tinay, a journalist working for the Emirates News Agency in Dubai, to join her and be a partner with her in a business venture to offset the financial obligations of the political campaign of 1986 in Sudan.

1.4

BETWEEN KHARTOUM AND PARIS
A TALE OF TWO CITIES

A SUDANESE IN PARIS: DR. MANSOUR KHALED

THE DILEMMA OF THE INTELLECTUAL AND
POWER IN AFRICA AND THE ARAB WORLD

"It is the job of thinking people not to be
on the side of the executioners."
Albert Camu

While in Paris 1968-1969 as a diplomat, I followed the political developments in Sudan through the media. Like many of my friends, as someone who was on the first lines of the glorious October 21st, 1964 revolution, I was naturally disappointed in and unhappy with the partisan and personality clashes of the politicians and the futile squabbles of the political parties, and especially those of the Umma party between Sadiq El-Mahdi and his uncle El-Hadi El-Mahdi. I felt the development challenges that the country faced were serious enough to make the politicians more responsible. They should reign in their egos and personal interests to do what was best for the country and focus on serving the country rather than waste their energy in politicking. To do something about this, I felt that I needed to return to the country to do whatever I could to put things right. I thought that I could be more useful to serving the country if I could contribute through sharing my perspective by speaking and writing and help promote a successful democratic governance experience, rather than working as a diplomat in Paris.

I wrote to the Ustaz Gamal Mohammed Ahmed, then Secretary General of the Ministry of Foreign Affairs requesting a transfer to headquarters in Khartoum. I was granted the transfer and returned to the country in February 1969. I did this while many of my diplomatic colleagues envied my posting in Paris and would have liked to be in my place. I always believed in causes that aim at serving a greater common good of society not just my personal success and that our country deserved better. Indeed, like most of us, I still do. Because I felt that change was better than stagnation, and that life was all about change. I also felt, intuitively, and still do, that power corrupts and that absolute power corrupts absolutely, and that the status quo everywhere is always prone to these human tendencies and therefore is amenable to improvement. If not jolted, it has a tendency to be part of the problem rather than part of the solution.

Many of us who were disenchanted with the traditional parties in those days were influenced by the revolutionary political mutations in the Middle Eastern and African regions. The success of the Egyptian Free Military Officers Movement's coup d'état, led by Mohamed Naguib, of Sudanese origin, and later on by Jamal Abdul Nasser, acted as a model to bring change to a stagnant, reactionary political and cultural environment in the Nile Valley and beyond.

My participation in the May 1968 Student Revolution at the Sorbonne in Paris, my enthusiastic opposition to the American War in Vietnam and support for the Civil Rights and Peace Movement in the United States were backdrops of my decision to support Numeiry's coup d'état. So from May of 1969 to July of 1971 I was involved with this new experiment as a civil servant as chief of Staff to Dr. Mansur Khalid, who I met during my Paris studies while he worked in the United Nations Educational Scientific and Cultural Organization (UNESCO). Our relationship deepened during my work as a Sudanese diplomat in Paris. Mansur Khalid was chosen to be the new regime's Minister of Youth, Sports, Social and Religious Affairs.

Dr. Mansur Khalid is an avid reader and a towering Sudanese researcher and a prolific writer. Disappointed by his experience with the Numeiri dictatorship of which he was one of its leaders, and after Numeiri's downfall through a popular uprising in April 1985, he joined Dr. John Garang and went on to be a member of the Political Bureau of the Sudan People's Liberation Movement (SPLM) and an advisor to its late President, Dr. John Garang. At Mansur's request, the Sudanese Foreign Ministry loaned me to the Ministry of Youth, and I was served between 1970 to 1971 his chief of staff.

This was a privileged vantage point to observe the way the new regime went about public policy, change and governance. I quickly saw the gap between the public rhetoric and the actual policies. I didn't like what I saw. I admit that I made a mistake in accepting to continue my public service under a dictatorial government that came to power through a military coup d'état. Alas and like most of us and in hindsight, I believe that I acted on emotion and opportunity rather than on reason and principle. Nimeiri revealed himself to be intolerant of perspectives other than his own. There is always a big difference between the promises of politicians when they need popular support and their actual behavior in administering the affairs of the state. I was a close observer of the Nimeiri government. Their actions angered me and acting on that anger, I supported Col. Hashim El-Atta's July 1971 coup d'état against Numeri. What tempers this mistake a little is the limited choice we had between incompetent partisan, civil, and feudal political elites and the military.

Numieri had stripped Col. Hashim El-Atta, Col. Babikir al-Nur and Major Faruk Hamdallah from their membership of the leadership of the Revolutionary Council, because of differences of opinion, which I felt was unjust. They were all officers I came to respect.

The three in turn wanted to take the government back from Numieri. Although all three plotted the events, Babikir al-Nur and Hamdallah were both in London at the time of the coup. Osman had gone there for medical treatment and Hamdallah went with him. It turned out to be one of a few miscalculations in their strategy. The other was the blatant embrace of the communist party. Although al-Atta denied there would be a strong influence of communist party principles, the rallies held after the coup, although sparse, were mainly seen as pro communist. There were shouts of a "red revolution" as part of the rallies being held. Sudanese citizens saw the pro-communist stance as an affront to their sensibilities. Muslims in the North and Christians in the South both saw communism tied directly to atheism. The people wanted a nationalist movement, not a communist one.

Africa and the Middle East: Looking for Answers
Victims of Colonialism and the Cold War
Coup d'Etats Masquerading as Revolutions

"When the elephants fight, it is the grass below that suffers" says an African proverb. These events took place during the peak of the Cold War, so there were already tensions in the region regarding the Soviet Union and their communist policies. In particular, Egyptian President Anwar Sadat and Libyan leader Col. Muammar Gaddafi objected to the potential Soviet presence in that part of Africa. Sadat authorized troops south of Khartoum to resist any attempts to spread the coup any further south. Gaddafi went a step further. Hamdallah and Babikir al-Nur attempted to get back into the country from

England. Their flight was met by Libyan jets and forced to land before reaching the Sudan. Both were arrested and detained. Although al-Atta was still in control, his hold on power was tenuous. Within a few hours of the Libyan action, troops loyal to Numeiri engaged al-Atta and his men, and he was defeated and captured, as well.

From Hashim to Hashim

Although I have always been in opposition to the extremes, I felt as though al-Atta would be the better choice for the country. I felt he and his friends were more authentic and had the people's' best interest at heart. After his takeover, I heard al-Atta speak about his plans on television and wanted to be supportive of his efforts. I drove to the radio station and asked his supporters if he needed volunteers to help achieve his goals. I was told no, but I left them something I had written to show al-Atta my support. On the way home, I heard some familiar words on the car radio. They had taken my statement and were reading it. Since we had one national radio station, more than a few people heard my statement, including Numeiri and his supporters.

My statement is popularly known in Sudan under the title "From Hashim to Hashim" and was portrayed by some superficial, lightweight commentators and by my detractors as an opportunistic gimmick to please the newcomers and to access power. To me it was a genuine and a serious intellectual input to the ongoing debate on our governance crisis, which is still occurring today. After congratulating al-Atta in succeeding in taking over, I went on to say, "This movement could usher a new beginning for societal renewal and progress, such that any one who is serious about leading for change in the Sudan should do so with total respect and deep awareness of the essence of Sudanese history and culture." These were the criteria by which I judged the Numeiri Experiment. It was, at the same time, an objective warning to al-Atta that he better deliver change for the people. So it was an intellectual contribution that was rooted in speaking the truth to the people in power and had nothing to do with political opportunism.

This story reflects the dilemma of the tenuous relationship between the intellectual and those in power, generally and especially in Africa and in the Muslim and Arab worlds. It seems unfathomable to me that society invests in education and that the universities produce citizen-intellectuals, but it is intolerant of their intellectual pronouncements and public statements. All I was doing was peacefully expressing my point of view based on my own knowledge. I was not driving a tank or taking a gun to threaten anybody. It was my duty and my way of contributing to solving the issues.

Once the coup was thwarted, there was a manhunt for all of the people who supported al-Atta in any way, shape or form. In the four days after the coup ended, members of the communist party and al-Atta supporters were rounded up. Hamdallah, Babikir al-Nur, al-Atta, Minister of Southern Affairs, Joseph Garang and Secretary General of the Communist Party, Abdel Khaliq Mahjub were among those who were executed on July 28 on the allegations that they played a role in overthrowing the government. I met my nephew, Col. Faisal Abbass, who worked for the Sudanese security agency at the time, at a family wedding in Khartoum North. Feisal took me aside and informed me that my name was on a list of people to be arrested because of the statement I had made. It had been read over the national radio many times by now. He told me that he told his Intelligence colleagues that they didn't need to arrest me, and that he would tell me to report to the authorities so I could turn myself in. Unlike a number of people who went underground to hide, I decided to turn myself in.

Although I was not executed, I did not completely escape the backlash. In the post-coup atmosphere, no one who was leftist or communist wanted to go anywhere near a police officer. I was comfortable with the stance I had taken and what I said. I believed I didn't do anything wrong. I expressed my opinion and the Government had a problem with it. That was what I had to deal with now.

Given the limited timeframe, I tried to get my affairs in order as best as I could. Once the wedding reception was over, I went back to my apartment, called for a meeting with my younger sister, Sayda Mustafa El-Tinay, a faculty of arts students at University of Khartoum at the time, and made the necessary arrangements with regards to my family responsibilities towards my mother and sister. I prepared a small backpack and then went to the Ministry of Interior and told them that I was the Hashim El-Tinay that they were looking for. I did not know whether the officer in charge was surprised by my insanity to deliver myself to the police who were hunting for anyone who expressed opposition to the regime and people like me or was impressed by my courage to face up to my actions. I did it because I didn't think that I was a criminal. All I did was make a statement supporting an action. So the officer was respectful and treated me to a cool cup of lemon juice and coffee and even a sandwich. He felt touched I had faith that no harm would come to me. The offering of tea and a sandwich allowed him to show his human side despite having to do what he was told. When the Kober prison car was ready, I was asked to sit in the back seat and driven directly to the prison.

I remember the drive wasn't very long so it didn't give me a lot of time to think about my circumstances. I don't remember being nervous. Even after we crossed over the Blue Nile Bridge between Khartoum and Khartoum North, which was the last barrier before getting to the prison's gates, I felt at peace. I firmly believe growing up in a home that emphasized a belief in God was a factor. I did what I did and said what I said acting on what I knew and on a noble purpose to serving the common good through ideas as I saw it. I was at peace with that. For the rest what will be, will be. You become resigned to leaving your circumstances in the hands of a higher power. In life many people think that they can control everything in their life, but believers humbly know that they are not in control. That in the end the Maker of this complicated, magical, beautiful and oftentimes messy world because of the three cancers that Martin Luther King spoke about racism, militarism and greed as well as ignorance and man's cruelty to man, alone has got the "whole world in His hand".

1.5

IN SUDAN KOBER PRISON:

"You cannot buy the revolution. You cannot make the revolution. You can only be the revolution. It is in your spirit, or it is nowhere."

— Ursula K. Le Guin, The Dispossessed

GENESIS OF A DEEPER CONSCIOUSNESS AND A QUEST FOR THE LIBERATION OF THE HUMAN SPIRIT

"WHILE IN A DEMOCRACY WORDS CAN MAKE YOU A PRESIDENT (BARACK OBAMA), IN DICTATORIAL AND TYRANNICAL SYSTEMS WORDS CAN EITHER GET YOU KILLED OR SEND YOU TO JAIL. IF YOU STOP TALKING YOU STOP LIVING. SO KEEP TALKING ANYWAY", HASHIM EL-TINAY (THE AUTHOR).

The car finally arrived at the gates of Kober Prison in Khartoum North. The high walls of the prison evoked the sensation of being deprived of one's freedom. The officials checked me in, took my driver's license and gave me a number. They led me down a corridor, and after a long walk, we arrived at the housing area. The housing area had big dorm like rooms that held 20 prisoners. There were no beds, which meant the dirt floors would be my less than comfortable bed. The officials gave me two blankets, one to use as a mattress and the other as a cover.

It was a relief when I met so many other intellectuals and activists representing all points of view in the Sudanese political landscape. The communists in the group were quick to ask me why I was jailed, even though I was supportive of Numeiri and was not a communist. I told them I was relieved to be there with them. The Sudan, back then, was a big prison with unruly and out-of-control soldiers armed to the teeth, who were on a manhunt. This prison was the only free and safe place in Sudan and where I wanted to be.

Apart from sleeping on the floor, being denied my basic human rights and barely being kept alive, I was definitely saved by my spiritual grounding, intellectual curiosity and my quest for understanding. We all walked for exercise. I used this time to engage in conversation with colleagues with different perspectives and different political, religious and social persuasions. Each day I chose a different person to engage. The diversity of the group gave me the chance to learn about many different disciplines and philosophies. Several people stand out among my prison group.

Professors Osama Abdelrahman El-Noor, an archeologist and the director of the Sudan Museum and Farouk Mohamed Ibrahim, a plant pathology specialist lecturer at the University of Khartoum, Salah Hassan, a High Court Judge, Ali Mohammed Khair, a science lecturer at the university of khartoum and Khalid Hassan El-Tom stood out. Having studied law and became a diplomat, I was curious to learn about their areas of academic and professional training which were different from mine. Although it was interesting to learn about their rich experiences, our most important discussions revolved around Sudanese history, regional and international politics and their social and economic problems and issues. Ibrahim was active in the reform movement well beyond our time together at Kober. It was the first of a few imprisonments he suffered through. The best-known imprisonment came later in 1989 when he disappeared for 12 days. A fellow professor who was a government henchman assisted in his kidnapping. He was taken to one of the infamous "ghost houses." These are clandestine spots where political prisoners are taken to be beaten and tortured outside of the legal prison system. His was accused of being a marxist and that he refused to stop teaching the theory of evolution. These conversations, which took place while we were having our morning or evening walks, were as informative as educational.

PRISON AND THE PASSION FOR LIBERATION

I had plenty of time to delve into reading, prayer, and I even had begun to teach French to some of my colleagues. Occasionally, I participated in organizing forums and discussions on the Sudanese governance crisis. I also organized entertainment through songs that were sung by the two famous icons of Sudanese music, Mohamed El-Amin and Mohamed Wardi. Wardi was considered one of the best singers in Africa. The Wadi Halfa native, from ancient Nubia in Northern Sudan, sang in both Arabic and Nubian languages. Wardi was considered one of the best singers in Africa. The Wadi Halfa native, from ancient Nubia in Northern Sudan, sang in both Arabic and Nubian languages. He played a few instruments, but was probably best known for performing with a Tambour. The Tambour is a stringed instrument with a long neck, similar in appearance to the Banjo. Although his subject matter ranged from romance to folklore, he was jailed for some of the political songs he recorded. He passed away in February 2012 just five months short of his 80th birthday.

One night five months into my imprisonment, the lights came on after lights out. It had only happened a few times during my stay. This time the guards shouted my name and told me I was free to go. I could go home. After any amount of time in jail most would have felt relief. For me it was a mixed feeling. It might seem strange to some that not leaving would even be an issue for consideration, but there was another side. It was true that the lights had only come on a few times while I was in Kober. Each time it was to set a prisoner free. The problem was that not all of those prisoners made it home. There were a few instances where release was a death sentence. As the freed prisoner made his way back into the world he ended up shot in the head and left in a ditch to die. So, besides being ambivalent about leaving people behind, there was no guarantee of my safe arrival home.

My Kober imprisonment experience was like a university of life where I had tapped into my inner resources, physical, moral, spiritual and cultural and discovered with my other co-prisoners of conscience the hidden and formidable power that comes from the liberation of the Human Spirit

I am glad to have been able to fruitfully use the time in jail to learn as much as I could. I considered every colleague as a rare resource to get to know better and learn his story. I was blessed to have succeeded in cultivating a number of good and lasting friendships and learned from some of the brightest minds in the country. I called on some of those minds, who were members of a council of wise prisoners of conscience when I received the order to leave Kober at one o'clock in the morning, if it was safe to leave at night or wait until the morning. They assessed the situation, clarified the issues and after a short deliberation, the majority of that group decided that they believed it would be safe for me to go in the dark of night. I thanked them for helping me to make the decision, collected my things from the supervisor's office and left.

I would learn later that I was never really in any danger. Once things had calmed down after the attempted coup, Nimeiri and his assistants began to sort out the who's who and the level of participation of those associated with the brief takeover. Some believe that Nimeiry had inquired about me and was the one who said that he knew that I was neither a communist nor a conspirator and ordered that I be freed right away. The most precious I learnt in Kober prison is that it is a great philosophy to remain calm and adopt, in situations of severe stress and adversity, an attitude of someone who transforms challenges into opportunities. A prison's limitation of our movement must not strip us of our liberty to think, dream, imagine and liberate our spirit. This is how the abundant time in prison can become a precious resource that can be invested in learning, education, research, reflection, prayer and, with hope, in planning for a new life after prison.

THE PURSUIT OF HAPPINESS: FROM CAREER TO CALLING?
Feelings, Thoughts, Words And Deeds Have Consequences

"Always go too far, because that's where you'll find the truth"
Albert Camu

The Nimeiri regime finally allowed me to go back to work after the tempest calmed down and the Sudanese Pharaoh General Numeiri had finally awakened to the fact that I wasn't a communist afterall. I returned to my work as a diplomat at the Sudanese Ministry of Foreign Affairs. I received four months worth of salary. My friend and boss, Dr Khalid, became the Minister of Foreign Affairs and invited me to be his Chief of Staff at the Ministry. I politely declined and made it clear to him that my ideas before and after my sejour in Kober prison had remained the same. I told him that I did not believe in this regime and that I would be leaving the country for good, to live in exile and work for a real change to take place. Ambassador Fakhr El Deen Mohamed saw to my transfer to the Sudanese Embassy in Bonn, Germany. The Ambassador there, Muzamil Ghandour, was a military man and did not want me. I suppose he thought I was a troublemaker. So I ended up being posted as First Secretary at the Sudanese Embassy in Lagos, Nigeria where I had the pleasure of joining the embassy team that included Ambassador Mubarak Osman Rahma, El-Fakki and Omar Alim. However, this was a tactical choice to quietly and discreetly find a way to exile. The prison experience settled the tension I had about deciding which way to go. Stay as a career diplomat who becomes a pawn of a questionable system, or follow my passion and calling to use my gifts and advocate for a better Sudan and a better world. That was where I found a deeper purpose and meaning for my life. So I decided to do my diplomatic job as best as I could but pursuing on the side my search for an exit strategy of liberation from the tyranny of slavery.

CONCLUSION

After having been released, I had to walk several miles in the dark toward my home. I knew the area pretty well so it made it a little less challenging to find my way. I could not say that it was a peaceful walk given my knowledge of what had happened to others. I eventually came upon a gas station. There was a cab sitting in the driveway. When I got into the passenger's side, I noticed he was asleep. I woke him and told him I needed him to take me home. Even though he was in a sleepy state, he said I looked as though I had just gotten out of Kober. When we arrived at the house, he turned to me and said he would not charge me. He said it was his contribution to my liberation from jail. Grassroots solidarity.

The lesson learnt from the iconic Nelson Mandela (Madiba's) 27 years of prison and the examples of many politicians and freedom fighters around the world is that no system has figured out how to imprison people advocating for a cause. Tyrants, repressive regimes and totalitarian governments may think that they can fight positive, noble and just ideas by putting people in jail. Ideas can only be won or lost on the merits or the demerits of other ideas. Ideas are not stoppable because they are like the rays of a clear morning sunshine and the breeze of Springtime. The reason why ideas cannot be imprisoned is the fact that they are rooted in the human mind, heart and most of all, spirit. While tyrants may be able to imprison the body, they cannot imprison the human spirit. Humanity's natural and unstoppable yearning for justice, dignity and freedom and its legitimate quest for the betterment of life, material and spiritual, has been the life force of innovation and progress across the ages.

No wonder that people from around the world are up in arms against the ruling elites perceived as self righteous and arrogant. The wanton violence unleashed by reactive military action against minority Muslim extremists who who are in bed with the war mongers in the West and the dumb wars in Muslim countries like Iraq and Libya and the messy destabilization of Syria resulted in the largest human migration since the second World War. The world seems to drift aimlessly, like an empty raft in the middle of a stormy sea. The shameful dysfunction of the the United States Congress since the election of President Barack Obama in 2008 and the uncanny stated public policy position of the Republican Party to make Obama's presidency a one term presidency. All of this and much more, explains the popular frustration and anger against Washington's establishment. Hence the success of the Bernie Sanders call for a grassroots movement for a social democratic revolution and Donald Trump's call to make America great again in the in America's unfolding 2016 presidential campaign. With the growing popular anger at establishments and what many see as corrupt tyrannical systems of governance that are rigged in favor of the 1% at the expense of the disappearing Middle Class and the impoverished 99%, I believe that we arrived at a moment of truth and we need to absolutely have the humility and the audacity to admit our failings and innovate a new vision suitable for the 21st century. A paradigm shift rooted in human equality, peace and solidarity is necessary. Time to radically change the culture from one of fear and violence to one of trust and peace.

Conclusion

My experiences at the University of Khartoum taught me that when people are united around a clear vision for change and are determined to work together to realize it, and especially if they are united by a noble, moral and clear vision, mission and goal, focused on serving the common good, they usually succeed. On the other hand, when people are in it just for themselves and are beholden to partisan and lobby driven agendas of racism, militarism and greed and thus divided by small, immoral and cynical "winner-takes-all" politics, they lose sight of any vision, mission and goal, and they are doomed to fail. We are not living on separate islands. We are living in a connected world. This principle was further enhanced as I was privileged to explore and travel the world.

This has become today Bernie Sanders' refrain in the ongoing 2016 presidential campaign who inspired millions of Americans to join his vision of a revolution to liberate American politics from being bought by money and free it from the bondage of the Wall Street millionaires and billionaires, perceived as agents of racism, militarism and greed.

Chapter Two

EUROPE: CONSCIOUSNESS

PARIS:

THE SECOND FRENCH REVOLUTION 1968

THE MAI 1968 SORBONNE STUDENT CONNECTION

In 1965 after graduating from law school, I joined the Sudanese diplomatic service. After passing two rigorous tests, I was given the choice between a the Sudanese United Nations Mission in the city that does not sleep, New York or go for a post graduate study of diplomacy and French language in the city of light, Paris. The two years Paris scholarship from the French Government involved a rigorous academic program administered through the Sorbonne affiliate the International Institute of Public Administration (IAAP). Our group of five young Sudanese diplomats learned French language and culture, as well as French, Western and international social dynamics during our years as students-diplomats. It was here that I feasted on all what the city of light offered in the various areas of music, theatre, writing, journalism, political activism and peace advocacy. Little did I know that this experience would serve me for the rest of my life.

A Strategic Choice: New York or Paris?
The United Nations or the Sorbonne?

When trying to decide where to go the Paris scholarship opportunity was timely and the best I could have hoped for. Having a penchant for research and intellectual pursuits, I did toy with the idea of becoming a lecturer at the faculty of law. However, I dismissed that idea when I thought more deeply about and critiqued the curriculum as being mostly rooted in the English Common law and culture rather than Sudanese law and culture. Aware of France's colonization of some African countries and that the French language was one of the official languages of the African Union and the United Nations, it seemed logical that studying French, diplomacy and public administration in Paris was the best I could do to prepare myself to continue my adventure (see the chapter about a Sudanese in the world) of taking on the world. Also, geographically, Paris and France didn't seem as far from the Sudan as was New York and the United States. We heard many stories about the strife black people were facing in the United States, especially lynching in the south. Even though I had reservations about the dark colonial and violent French history in Africa and especially in Algeria, it did not seem like my life would be as threatened as much there as it would have been in the United States. After some prayer and deliberation and discussions with my parents and family as well as some of my teachers and friends, I decided for the lights of Paris over the electricity of the Big Apple. In essence that was really a choice between heart and mind. I have a passion for learning and was always wary of systems that were created to serve the powers that be disguised as serving the common good. So I chose a path that enabled me to pursue more education. Knowledge, in my family, and in the Sudanese, African, Arab and Muslim culture, is considered a supreme value (remember the Prophet's hadith where he encouraged Muslims to seek knowledge wherever they can find it, even if in China). Besides the language and other courses on diplomatic history, international relations, international social and economic development and the like, there was the seductive lure of French culture and civilization that we have read about in the works of the famous Egyptian writers such as Taha Hussein, Naguib Mahfouz, Al-Tahtawi, Mohammed

Abdu and the like. No wonder then that I ended up falling in love with Paris, France and Anne, my French wife for eight years. But that is another story.

The Paris of the mid to late 60s was a haven for revolutionary students who used their knowledge and awareness to challenge the status quo and their parents at home and their governance systems. As a young diplomat-scholar, I took my Parisian sojourn very seriously by dedicating my time to studies. I would use cultural awareness activities as a break. Going to the movies at Rue Saint Jacques, Boulevard Saint Michel and Boulevard Saint Germaine were some of those activities. It was in these relaxed moments that I met someone who, even though I didn't know it when we first met, would eventually be one of my most satisfying relationships I had. It began as a pure friendship. I met Anne while we were students at the Sorbonne. We lived in the campus of Nanterre University-Paris 10 students' dormitory on the outskirts of Paris. Our group of friends composed of students from Algeria, Senegal, Ivory Coast, Benin, Tunisia, Morocco, Cameroon, and Egypt who would meet on weekends to go to the movies in the Sorbonne Latin Quarter in downtown Paris.

Upon completion of the two years at the Sorbonne, I returned to the Sudan to await a permanent assignment. On the basis of my academic record and character, the Sudanese Ministry of Foreign Affairs decided that it would be good if I could join the Sudanese embassy in Paris, France as my first full time diplomatic position.

Upon my return I found myself engaging the French government by day and assisting French students protesting their government at night. I advised some of the leaders of the 1968 revolutionary movement in Paris. The leaders just happened to be classmates of mine during my time at the Sorbonne. My own experience with the 1964 Sudanese Student led Revolution gave me an expertise that enabled me to pass on to the French students. I considered myself as giving back to Paris, to France and to our never-ending quest for liberation from what we perceived as the exploitation and modern day slavery imposed on us by the tyranny of unjust governance systems.

Shaking hands and having a picture with President Charles de Gaulle when I first arrived at my diplomatic post in Paris in the winter of 1967 did not stop me from helping my revolutionary buddies plan ways to disrupt his government, perceived as failing in its mandate to serve the wellbeing of all the French people. The revolt started as student protests against the government threatening to close the Sorbonne and expelling university students. It eventually led to a series of strikes that involved 11,000,000 French citizens. In addition to the success of the movement, I derived some personal satisfaction in another way. For years, Europeans had come to Africa to try to tell us how to do things. This was an opportunity for a Sudanese who was both of Arab and African culture to advise them on how to achieve their goals. A genesis of sorts for a South North grassroots cooperation harbinger of a popular and better organized action for societal change in the direction of the legitimate aspiration of all the people and their yearning for liberation from elitist and bureaucratic exploitation and slavery.

We'd take the Paris Metro to Boulevards Saint Michel and Saint Germaine in the Latin Quarter to eat our favorite North African couscous dishes at the Chez Hamadi Tunisian Restaurant. Then, we'd hang out in cafes or go to the movies. Anne and Mustafa, her Tunisian boyfriend, were part of that group. What was interesting about her was that she was knowledgeable, sociable and well organized. She spoke both English and Spanish, was elegant and always dressed neatly. I couldn't help but notice that right away. She was daring compared to the other girls. She wasn't afraid to be who she was no matter what anyone thought about her. That's a virtue in my book. I also appreciated that she was into music. She introduced me to Jacques Brel, Edith Piaf, Francoise Hardy, Juliette Greco, Georges Brassens and Jimi Hendrix. She also introduced me to the Montmartre's Painters Village and the works of Picasso.

Her father was a German priest who opposed Hitler's Nazism and her mother was an Italian in opposition to Mussolini's Fascism. They both ended up as refugees in Paris. So their union in Paris was the result of leaving tyrannical situations in their countries of origin. They were people who were struggling for their freedom. I could truly relate to their stories, even more so many years later, as my own experiences and struggles against tyranny and dictatorship in Sudan mirrored theirs.

When our time at the Sorbonne ended in 1968 we went our separate ways. While she went to work for the French embassy in Ouagadougou, the capital of Burkina Faso, in West Africa, I bounced through my various life experiences in Khartoum, Lagos, Geneva and Washington, DC.

Chapter Three

AMERICA: A RUDE AWAKENING

TOWARDS THE SECOND AMERICAN REVOLUTION

FROM OBAMA'S FRUSTRATION TO BERNIE SANDERS REVOLUTION

A SUDANESE-AMERICAN IN WASHINGTON
From World Banker, to
Peace Advocate, to Homeless, to
President Elect and to Honorary
Member of President Obama's Kitchen Cabinet

Writing a New Chapter

Contrary to what the extremists and the demagogues of all stripes that feel more comfortable barricading themselves into superficial and partial ghettoized and exclusivist dogma and choosing the easier wrong instead of the harder right, we are starting to realize that each individual has multiple identities. In this 21st century age of globalization it is definitely a blessing to belong to two communities, countries, cultures, continents and races etc. As someone who has the privilege of having dual nationality, I felt blessed to have been able to leave Khartoum and come back to Washington, DC, the capital of my new country and home in the New World in the United States, after my disappointing one year (2007-2008) experience in Sudan.

During those first few days in Sudan in 2007, I received a kind invitation to attend an event about the presidential campaign in the US at the American embassy in Khartoum. I had an opportunity to advocate for the candidacy of the young and charismatic Chicago Senator Barack Hussein Obama, a man whom I had gotten into an argument with my African-American ex-wife about, because of her remark that he was not black enough. I did so despite my reservation about a rigged and a corrupt system that is, alas, rooted into racism, militarism and greed.

So when I returned to Washington, D.C., in August 2008, I immediately signed in as a volunteer for the Obama-Biden campaign in McLean, Virginia.

I did this although I was homeless and survived thanks to the various shelters for the Washington homeless. I suppose I followed my heart rooting for the big dream in me for peace in America and for peace in the world. Fast forward to the ongoing presidential campaign, this is why I am now rooting for the vision that Bernie Sanders started to share with America and the world since he declared running for president in June 2016.

This was my opportunity to really appreciate, celebrate and embrace fully my new country and the privileges of being an American citizen. I did this in 2008 and in 2012 with dedication, enthusiasm and joy. Despite the drying up of work opportunities as an independant contractor and an Arabic language interpreter and my meager financial means, I made sacrifices to be able to donate whatever money savings I could find to the cause. I also generously volunteered my time and energy and phone-banked for Obama and Biden as well as for the Democratic party candidates up and down the ticket at the Democratic National Women's Club as well as the Democratic National Committee (DNC).

I knocked on doors and canvassed door to door in Virginia. Later I became a founding member of the Democratic Party's grassroots organization, Organizing for Action (OFA). When I finally found a place to stand on close to the Campus of George Washington University in the strategically located Foggy Bottom neighborhood, I decided to lay anchor, focus on research, study and refining my peace vision and sharing it as best as I knew how and went to work.

My new neighborhood was ideal and strategically located for what I wanted to do. It was one block away from the George Washington University library, a few stations on the direct line of the orange and blue metro to the library of Congress, a few blocks from the Kennedy Center, the Watergate, the Washington Harbor, the Potomac River, Rock Creek Park, the National Mall, the White House, the World Bank, the International Monetary Fund, K Street, the State Department, Georgetown University, the Marriott and Fairmont Hotels etc. It was from here that I resumed my peace Quest advocacy activities. It was here that I reclaimed my peace voice and was embraced by the George Washington University students.

Inspired by what I was sharing with them they started an IPQI chapter at the university.

Reflecting on my life's journey I thought it was time to slow down, review, evaluate and reflect on the journey thus far. So naturally I reorganized my priorities. I started focussing on reading, research and the project of writing this memoir since 2011. I also invested some of my time to learn how to use Facebook, Twitter, Linkedin and other social media platforms. To share the fruits of my intellectual growth and learning with the members of my new community, I organized a Peace Quest Conversation at Saint Mary's Court the second Wednesday of each month. Beside my efforts to share my vision at the community grassroots level, I continued trying to speak truth to power by expressing myself through my blog, my website and the various Social Media. I also wrote and sent letters directly to president Barack Obama.

A year earlier in July 2013 I received a certificate from the Democratic National Committee (DNC) signed by its Chief of Staff and President Obama that I was appointed by president Obama as an honorary member of president Obama's Kitchen Cabinet. I also received a number of personal mementoes from First lady Michelle Obama and President Barack Obama, expressing gracefully their appreciation of my unwavering support and commitment to our democratic cause and our push for social and economic justice, equality and human dignity by reigning in the evils of racism, militarism and greed in America and in the world.

Thanks to my grassroots community volunteering work and my monthly conversation on peace, the Saint Mary's Court Management acknowledged my efforts and awarded me various volunteer awards. The leaders in the community also took notice. When it was time to elect a new executive board, they invited me to run for president of the Saint Mary's Court Residents Association. I ran competing with two American born residents, one black and one white, whereas I am a new immigrant naturalized in 2002 who has dual nationality. I enjoyed the democratic process and when the ballots were counted, I obtained 60% of the votes and each of the other candidates obtained 20% of the popular vote. So I was elected president of my new community's resident's association in June 2014. That was how I went from being a World Bank staff, an entrepreneur, a peace advocate, a homeless person in Washington, D.C to president elect. You can read the political platform statement on which I ran as well as my victory speech below or in the appendix pages at the end of the book.

So we first flew from beautiful Washington, DC, on the Potomac River and capital of the United States of America to beautiful Beirut on the Mediterranean and capital of Lebanon. Despite the skepticism of the Lebanese media given the drumbeat of war coming out of Washington, the American embassy in Beirut put together excellent public affairs, media and community outreach programs. We were involved in different community conversations and activities with Lebanese Christian, as well as Muslim leaders. Those conversations were open, frank and candid.

The most notable one was being invited to a Town Hall TV show to discuss Arab-Muslim-American relations after 9/11 as visiting Muslim American guests by Zaven Kouyoumdjian of Future TV. Zaven is a high profile Lebanese journalist who is rated as the best talk show journalist in the Middle East. His widely watched and popular Future TV's Sire Wenfatahit Live show is the highest rated TV show in the Middle East. In 2005, Newsweek rated him as one of the 42 most influential personalities in the Arab World. The idea was to use the opportunity of our visit on the wake of the tragic events of 9/11 and our good will to engage a people-to-people dialogue, rather than the seemingly ineffective and failed communication between the official political and bureaucratic institutions that were leading us to another war, and have a larger public conversation on Arab Muslim American relations. The invitees from the Lebanese side included the dean, professors and finalist students of the School of Journalism, Media and Public Affairs of the American University of Beirut. We were all together in a town hall format. The show was in Arabic.

When official America teaches about democracy nobody listens because they think it's a hoax. When someone like me who has roots there and has a story that people respect speaks, that carries a lot of weight. My journey is truth and evidence to the importance of having a voice and using it to give voice to the voiceless who are enslaved by the tyrants, the terrorists and the religious extremists. Ignorance is rampant and people can be manipulated by the people who control the media. That's why I call for liberation. It was recognition for my journey. I am a misfit in my native country and the powers that be put me in jail because I speak my mind. I was lucky because many of my friends were killed. Here I found a country that not only accepts me, but sees value in my character and in my story and embraces that by giving me the honor of being a citizen and being, for a brief moment in history, a representative of the country's civil society.

When Zaven asked me his provocative question about being a successful American and forgetting the Sudan I told him that I could be his father in age. I told him that I am proud to be a Sudanese-American who is Muslim, a global citizen, black, speaks Arabic, was raised in the Sudan (which makes me Afro-Arab), and was educated at the University of Khartoum, the Sorbonne and the George Washington University in the United States. It was my love of country that forced me to go into exile refusing to participate in the dominate narrative and therefore, be part of the problem. As someone who dares to think out of the box, and as an innovator and a social entrepreneur, I was somebody who had ideas and ideas die in the absence of freedom. And yes I am happy to have found in America a country whose constitution guarantees me my basic human rights and freedoms that I was deprived of in the Sudan, and that I hope all the Sudanese, African and Arab people enjoy one day. Because this became my calling, I am someone who made sacrifices to maintain the authenticity and integrity of my calling.

Then I went on the offensive and told Zaven and his audience on the show, in Beirut, in the Arab world, that the Arab media should be discussing why Arab and Muslim intellectuals leave their native countries in droves and choose to live in America, Europe and the West? I added that it was because of the absence of fundamental human rights and basic freedoms without which ideas cannot flourish. It was a good exposure to the Arab media, albeit at the eleventh hour and in a legitimately suspicious and almost cynical environment of people who were convinced that a war was imminent anyway.

I tried to help people to focus on the promise of overcoming our predicament despite the objective limitations of our tyrants and the often shallow and short-term myopia of American foreign policy. We often get caught up in the distractions: the zero sum game of Blacks versus Whites, Christians and Jews versus Muslims, Africans versus Arabs etc. The cynical gatekeepers of power, who are themselves victims of their own choices to make a living, have mastered the art of divide and conquer; the art of manipulating the world through the word for their own gain. To continue on top, they revel in pitting us against each other all the time. Sometimes I felt it while talking to people. It was tough going, meeting the media and colleagues. Telling them we were Americans. When I spoke my mind in Sudan they put me in jail. When I went to America I wrote a candid letter to president Bush and told him exactly what I thought. Not only I was not put in jail, I got a letter from the President thanking me for my ideas. It's all about the voice.

That's what made it a little easier for me to address the people I was meeting and be heard. In Jordan I met with Prince El-Hassan Bin Talal, the uncle of King Abdullah and the brother of the late King Hussain. Besides being a descendant of Prophet Mohamed, Prince El-Hassan is a wise Muslim and Arab intellectual and thinker.

I first met him at an interfaith peace conference held in Amman a year before. He told me about his friendship with many Sudanese during his Oxford University days and especially with Professor Mohamed Omer Bashir, who was one of my mentors at the University of Khartoum. We had a dinner at his residence with his Pakistani wife and it was interesting to discover that most of the people cooking and serving the food were from the Sudan. We became friends and we write and share ideas with each other till today. So it was a nice way to see him again during this trip and reconnect with him. It also confirmed that like-minded people can shed all that could separate them and get on the same page.

Our objective was building bridges and helping people get out of the ghetto of the "us versus them" mentality. The State Department did the heavy lifting. They ran the operational side, the choice of countries and the in country logistics. We were using the embassies to create outreach to the communities. We met Christian and Muslim leaders. The department did all the nitty gritty of the program. We were American Muslim grassroots leaders of good will who wanted to engage in a people-to-people conversation with our counterparts in Arab and Muslim countries of the Middle East. It was an exercise in people to people and public diplomacy, away from the objective limitations of bureaucracy and raw politics. It was just letting them know that as American Muslims, we are a free people whose freedom of thought, speech and worship that the American Constitution guarantees. Although the American government has its job to do, we as citizens don't always agree with what the government does. That was how we could get some kind of acceptance from the other side. We wanted them to know that just as they were struggling, we were struggling with our government. The people I spoke with were saying that I sounded like I was happy in America and wondered whether I forgot my country of origin, the Sudan.

It is often hard to separate out when you have entrenched positions. To them it was almost an either or proposition. It was as though I could not live and embrace my new home without completely forgetting about where I came from. That is a lie. I said I'm proud to have been raised and born in Sudan. And I'm equally as proud to have found a place like America whose constitution guarantees my freedom of thought, expression and worship, the absence of which drove me into exile, in the first place. Unlike most countries of Africa, the Arab and Muslim worlds and the Middle East, in America I am free to think what I want, speak what I want, and worship as I want. I asked why do your freethinkers move to the US and Europe? In many cases voices of dissension are stifled in Middle Eastern and African countries. In order to make yourself known, you need to know that you can voice your opinion. Even though you will never see complete compliance with all your viewpoints realized, it is vital just to know you can say it without severe retribution. That's what America and Europe has. That is the secret of the success of their economies and governance models.

This trip was just before the infamous declaration by Colin Powell before the United Nations and the whole wide world that Iraq had chemical weapons and George W. Bush's declaration of war against Iraq, which many of us were against and tried to warn against. As a community and aware of the American culture's fascination with violence and war games, we saw war coming. This, though, did not prevent us from doing what we could to educate people on the negative long-term consequences of angry reactions and war.

Aside from my work with my non-profits, I was involved in many organizations in Washington, DC. Within the Center of American

Muslims for Understanding (CAMU), a grassroots civil society Muslim organization, my colleagues and I had spent several months in 2002 working with the State Department on an initiative to open up channels of communication and dialogue with community leaders for both Muslims and Christians in the Middle East and African nations. We believed the time we spent talking to our peers in other countries would at least be a step in the right direction. As a new American citizen, I thought it was my duty to go on behalf of my adopted country to see if our dialogue could move us toward a new paradigm in international relations. It also just happened to be the centerpiece of my philosophy on making the world a more peaceful place. Without dialogue there can be no relationship and therefore no understanding and our world will continue on the spiral of violence.

To me this impending military action was very, very disappointing. It was counter to what we were trying to start in our people to people diplomacy and our 2002 mission in the Middle East. We wanted to start a conversation that could take off with different communities in an effort to make engagement the bedrock for greater understanding. That was the whole idea; to take away the momentum of mistrust, mutual hatred, mutual anger and mutual demonization that was counterproductive and logically leads to violence. That's exactly what I wanted people to avoid. That's the logical outcome of not engaging in serious exchange. At that time I was an at-large Muslim Board Member of the InterFaith Conference of Metropolitan Washington (IFC), an umbrella organization for everybody who claims to believe in God. Its members included Christians, Muslims, Jews, Hindus, Buddhists, and Sikhs etc. It didn't matter what your belief was. The clear objective was to have a safe space for interreligious fellowship, dialogue and hopefully understanding and help make the world a better place. It was within IFC and other similar civil society organizations that we worked toward doing something at a grassroots level. We decided on a candlelight vigil on The Mall.

We wanted to bring things into perspective. We wanted to highlight the absurdity of wars and advocate for a renewal of the way we think and conduct conflicts, because popular wisdom teaches us that war is not the answer. Besides, didn't we have enough wars already? There was a walk from the Lincoln Memorial to the Vietnam Memorial. Then we had an event on the Vietnam Memorial where various speakers spoke against the war. There were also performers who performed against the war. There wasn't a stage or anything. We just wanted to bring people together around the idea of avoiding an unnecessary war.

I was excited and happy that people came out and had all these candles. It was a beautiful spectacle to behold. In some ways it was overwhelming. I felt empowered, especially coming from the background of being persecuted for expressing my ideas. It was a blessing to be in a country and be able to speak up and express my opinion without being persecuted for it. It was great to be with like-minded people. When you're bombarded everyday with television images advocating for war, you need to see another viewpoint. It was great to be in a different community. Another thing that crossed my mind was the feeling that this was a drop in the ocean compared to the larger community or people objecting to the war.

I wished everybody was there to experience it. I wanted to counteract the mainstream media and all the hype. We had a small island of well-intentioned people who cared, and who didn't want people to get hurt. We felt that was the duty of a government of the people, by the people and for the people. The general feeling was that some people are so full of themselves and so narcissistic, much like Donald Rumsfeld and Dick Cheney. They think they are good people and nobody else is. This is how they came across in the world media. It's not good.

When the event started everybody shared some of their thoughts. It was upbeat even though we knew war was inevitable. We made a statement, and we took a stand. It was a very diverse and eclectic group of people. There were Jews, Christians, Muslims, Palestinians, Arabs, Africans, and all different types of nationalities banding together against the war. That was the first time I met Egyptian journalist, feminist and author Mona El-Tahawy. She is a prolific writer, great public speaker and advocate for human rights. Since that time, she has been named Time Magazine's Person of the Year and was counted among Newsweek's Most Fearless People.

The legendary American folk singer and poet, the late Pete Seeger, sang. I became aware of his work during my Paris studies from 1966-1968 when he was an anti-Vietnam war protestor. We were both demonstrating against the war while I was at the Sorbonne. Peter, Paul and Mary were there and also performed. There were speeches and performances all in the spirit of peace. I was very happy and elated. Just the idea that we could be together and do what we were doing in a country whose constitution guaranteed our freedom of thought and expression and organization was wonderful. We were able to express our thoughts. That was great because of my background. The police were there to protect us, too. Not to persecute us, take us to jail or to shoot us like they have been doing in Sudan and many other places in Africa and the Middle East, regrettably by hijacking the state, or religion. This was my final coming to America moment. In the end experiences matter and we are better for it when the lessons learnt from those experiences inform our decisions.

Chapter 6

FROM OBAMA'S FRUSTRATION TO BERNIE SANDERS REVOLUTION
Swimming Against the Current:
Peace Advocacy: From Homelessness, to President Elect to Honorary Member of President Obama's Kitchen Cabinet

"In a Gentle Way You Can Shake the World",
Mahatma Ghandi

Contrary to what the extremists, the cynics and the demagogues of all stripes that feel more comfortable barricading themselves into superficial and partial ghettoized and exclusivist dogma and choosing the easier wrong instead of the harder right, we are starting to realize that each individual has multiple identities. In this 21st century age of globalization it is definitely a blessing to belong to two communities, countries, cultures, continents and races etc. As someone who has the privilege of having dual nationality, I felt blessed to have been able to leave Khartoum and come back to Washington, DC, the capital of my new country and home in the New World in the United States, after my disappointing one year (2007-2008) experience in Sudan.

During those first few days in Sudan in 2007, I received a kind invitation to attend an event about the presidential campaign in the US at the American embassy in Khartoum. I had an opportunity to advocate for the candidacy of the young and charismatic Chicago Senator Barack Hussein Obama, a man whom I had gotten into an argument with my African-American ex-wife about, because of her remark that he was not black enough. I did so despite my reservation about a rigged and a corrupt system that is, alas, rooted into racism, militarism and greed.

So when I returned to Washington, D.C., in August 2008, I immediately signed in as a volunteer for the Obama-Biden campaign in McLean, Virginia. I did this although I was homeless and survived thanks to the various shelters for the Washington homeless. I

suppose I followed my heart rooting for the big dream in me for peace in America and for peace in the world. Fast forward to the ongoing presidential campaign, this is why I am now rooting for the vision that Bernie Sanders started to share with America and the world since he declared running for president in June 2016.

This was my opportunity to really appreciate, celebrate and embrace fully my new country and the privileges of being an American citizen. I did this in 2008 and in 2012 with dedication, enthusiasm and joy. Despite the drying up of work opportunities as an independant contractor and an Arabic language interpreter and my meager financial means, I made sacrifices to be able to donate whatever money savings I could find to the cause. I also generously volunteered my time and energy and phone-banked for Obama and Biden as well as for the Democratic party candidates up and down the ticket at the Democratic National Women's Club as well as the Democratic National Committee (DNC).

I knocked on doors and canvassed door to door in Virginia. Later I became a founding member of the Democratic Party's grassroots organization, Organizing for Action (OFA). When I finally found a place to stand on close to the Campus of George Washington University in the strategically located Foggy Bottom neighborhood, I decided to lay anchor, focus on research, study and refining my peace vision and sharing it as best as I knew how and went to work.

My new neighborhood is ideal and strategically located for what I wanted to do. It was one block away from the George Washington University GWU-Foggy Bottom Metro station, the GWU-Gelman library, a few stations on the direct line of the orange and blue Metro to the library of Congress, the Supreme Court, Union Station, a few blocks from the Kennedy Center, the Watergate, the Washington Harbor, Georgetown, the Potomac River, Rock Creek Park, the Smithsonian Museums and the National Mall, the White House, the World Bank, the International Monetary Fund, K Street, the State Department, Georgetown University, the Marriott, the Westin, the Fairmont Hotels etc. It was from here that I resumed my peace Quest advocacy activities. It was here that I reclaimed my peace voice and was embraced by the George Washington University students.

Inspired by what I was sharing with them they started an IPQI chapter at the university.

Reflecting on my life, I felt that the time has come for me to slow down, review, evaluate critically and reflect on the journey thus far. The more I reflected the more I naturally reorganized my priorities. I started focussing on reading, research and the project of writing this memoir since 2013 after the publication of my first book by Amazon entitled: "Nile Sunrise" Winds of Revolution and Liberation in Africa and the MIddle East, the Case of Sudan, available on Amazon.com. I also invested some of my time to learn how to use the Social Media such as Facebook, Twitter, Linkedin, Pinterest, Instagram and other social media platforms to share the fruits of my intellectual growth and learning with the members of my new community and the world. I organized a Peace Quest Conversation at Saint Mary's Court the second Wednesday of each month that ran from 2010 until 2014. Beside my efforts to share my vision at the community grassroots level, I continued trying to speak truth to power, in the best manner, by expressing myself through my blog, my website and the various Social Media. I also wrote and sent letters directly to president Barack Obama (See appendix).

A year earlier in July 2013 I received a certificate from the Democratic National Committee (DNC) informing me that I was appointed by president Obama as an honorary member of president Obama's Kitchen Cabinet, signed by President Barack Obama and the DNC Chief of Staff. I also received a number of personal mementoes from President Barack Obama and First lady Michelle Obama, expressing gracefully their appreciation of my unwavering support and commitment and work to perfect the union by bettering our democracy and our push for social and economic justice, equality and human dignity by reigning in the evils of racism, militarism and greed in America and in the world.

Thanks to my grassroots community volunteering work and my monthly conversation on peace, the Saint Mary's Court Management acknowledged my efforts and awarded me various volunteer awards. The leaders in the community also took notice. When it was time to elect a new executive board, they invited me to run for president of the Saint Mary's Court Residents Association. I ran competing with two American born residents, one black and one white, whereas I am a new immigrant naturalized in 2002 who has dual nationality. I enjoyed the democratic process and when the ballots were counted, I obtained 60% of the votes and each of the other candidates obtained 20% of the popular vote. So I was elected president of my new community's resident's association in June 2014. That was how I went from being a World Bank staff, an entrepreneur, a peace advocate, a homeless person in Washington, D.C to president elect. You can read the political platform statement on which I ran as well as my victory speech below or in the appendix pages at the end of the book.

For more visit my website at:

http://www.hashimeltinay.com/

For more on my Peace Quest Blog visit:

http://hashim-peacequest.blogspot.com/

For more on my Peace Quest Foggy Bottom Conversations visit us on Youtube:

https://www.youtube.com/watch?v=KnGPwPbnvx

Conclusion

"The only way to deal with an unfree world is to
become so absolutely free that your
very existence is an act of rebellion."
Albert Camu

"The People who are crazy enough to think
that they can change the world are the ones who do"
Steve Jobs

As in the beginning was, is and will always be, the "WORD", so is, in the beginning was, is and will indeed always be good and evil. That is why the quality of communication was, is and will indeed always be key in determining the quality of human relations at all levels. Instead of going about life trying to impose our narratives on one another, it might be wiser to seek the truth about the narrative we uphold as our truth and engage with other people who are entitled to believe in other narratives. While a kind word and a smile can lead to understanding and possibly friendship and peace, a rude, and vulgar word and a mean attitude can lead to anger, misunderstanding, animosity, hatred and war. During my journey so far, I believe that thanks to the love of my family, the quality education I have had thanks to the Sudanese people, the generous hospitality I experienced and received during my travels all over the world, and the many genuine conversations and observations were the solid foundations of my life. My experience points to the promise of what is possible when different cultures, religions and civilizations meet, respectfully communicate and engage in healthy conversations that can lead to a deeper awareness, understanding, trust and friendship.

In this 21st Century of globalization we should practice humility admitting the fact that while we have accomplished great feats of technological exploits and wonders from starting by putting a man on the moon to putting a smart phone and the universe in a man's pocket, we are lagging behind in the lack of innovation in the social sciences. As human knowledge is dynamic, ever changing and relative, we need to critically ponder the whys of the widening gap between the spectacular advances in the innovation of technology and the falling behind of the social sciences and the dearth of audacious and novel ideas addressing our modern day societal challenges. We need to learn to practice listening more than talking. We need to learn the virtue of tempering our passion to share our perspective and do not let it trump our willingness to learn more about opposing perspectives, no matter how hard that was, is or will be.

The communication revolution brought about by the Social Media that finally democratized the flow and access to information and popularized knowledge ought to help all of us to stop barricading ourselves into our ghettos, or bubbles of illusionary comfort zones, acting as separate islands, no matter how successful, content or proud we might be of our race, ethnicity, governance systems, culture, religion or money etc. The more the environment in which we meet and operate is devoid of malice, the more an honest conversation can be life generating and constructive. Thank God for the United Nations charter which the UN bureaucrats who are supposed to be inspired by are still striving to concretize in reality! Despite Rwanda, Kosovo, Cambodia, Darfur, Palestine, Iraq, Afghanistan, Congo, and others, its conversations spared us, so far, from an all out Third World War.

I am grateful to a life that taught me lessons I was blessed to learn from my parents, my village elders, all my teachers old and young, my students and the virtue and the joys of giving through volunteering. This was nourished y my early involvement in extracurricular activities, my curiosity to discover, my passion to serve and help others by striving to do my part in improving myself and help to making the world, from my limited experience and perspective, a better place. All of this awareness continues to drive me to strive through research and reading towards a deeper consciousness and a higher level of an awakening that is my goal. This constitutes the bedrock of my optimistic philosophy, vision and faith in working for the advent of a liberation of the human spirit and the emergence of a new humanism.

Although I am indebted and grateful to my parents, teachers, friends and all human beings who helped me see the light, I know that my early encounter with the injustices that some people inflicted on other people have sown the seed of revolt in me. I find people who practice injustice of any kind against others as seriously and dangerously flawed and inhuman. My early involvement in volunteerism and activism showed me a way to do good and made a great difference and helped give a deeper meaning to my life. Those experiences taught me that the more we become aware of the light and darkness in the human soul, narrative, and accept its messy truth for what it really is, the more we can attain humility, objectivity and with a bit of luck, even the bliss of integrity. The more we seek, find and embrace the truth, the more likely that it will set us free.

Speaking truth to power is, however, a duty and a solemn responsibility of all amongst us who are blessed to have had the opportunity of a good education, had access to knowledge and have, as a result been fortunate enough to see the light. The more these people realize that their silence vis-a-vis tyrannical governance systems and wrongdoing is indeed acceptance, and stand up to expose it, the better our world will be. The more we take responsibility for our thoughts, words and actions, or lack thereof, the more we can deepen or lessen our awareness and be able to reigning in our worst demons, unleash our better angels and be, as Mahatma Gandhi said: "Be the change we want to see in the world".

Because only when we allow the flow of our God-given positive energy to help one another move forward can we hope to attain the mountaintop of our human awakening and the bliss of our inner peace. Such a process can only be attained through a more sincere, truth-seeking, patient, mature and pragmatic conversation, whose aim is truth, reaching common ground and building bridges of trust and compassion. Once we do that, we can then proceed to fixing the problems and challenges facing our broken human family, our broken human community, our broken neighborhood, our broken cities, hamlets, countries and our broken world.

In scholarly language, we are seeking to innovate and invent a new paradigm that can allow us to reach a new basis for a much needed new transformed 21st century humanism that can lead us away from racism, militarism, greed, fear, violence and wars to one of freedom, solidarity, social and economic justice, trust and peace. These are the necessary prerequisites for attaining social and economic justice, genuine freedom and human dignity. If we do all that, we might finally realize the big dream of creating heaven here on earth, instead of slipping, as we seem to be these days, toward an impending Armageddon. My ambition, as a thinker, advocate and change agent, was to dream the big dreams and add my voice to all the founders and shapers and teachers who preceded us. All those who, across the ages, who were compassionate, caring, loving and hopeful enough to dream the big dreams for all of us.

Dreams of a vision of societal transformation that is truly of the people, by the people and for the people. That of course could only be possible through the liberation of the human spirit impossible without a governance system that guarantees the fundamental human rights of freedom of thought, expression, universal healthcare, universal free college education, work, housing, respect of the rule of law and the separation of the legislative, judicial and executive powers i.e. a genuine democratic system of governance.

In my twenties as a law student at the University of Khartoum, now risking to be sold for the highest bidder by tyrannical and extremist fanatics who hijacked a peaceful people, a beautiful country and a great religion, I was a revolutionary social democrat. No wonder that I am having a blast these days following the 2016 presidential campaign from my Foggy Bottom base in Washington, D.C. I am naturally excited by Bernie Sander's call for a new American revolution and his vision for a social democratic America and world, that I share.

However, my public relations (PR) successes as a democrat during the Obama years (2008-2016), in reality, like most new immigrants to the United States of America, I was denied real access to the opportunities I deserved by the system's gatekeepers. So as a marginalized and barely tolerated democrat, despite all the time, energy and financial support I provided, and feeling powerless to do anything about it, I am amused to no end, like the enthusiastic millions on both sides of the political spectrum, by the fact that finally we found in Bernie Sanders, an American politician who gave us a voice.

Bernie Sanders: Making History Again in 2016

http://youtu.be/VbeuFczjg4U

Bernie Sanders vision resonated with many of us and especially with me, as I felt that he was someone who embraces my lifelong yearning, advocacy and work for a world of social, economic, racial and environmental justice and peace and who courageously mainstreamed these ideas in America's political discourse. Bernie Sanders happened to be an independent Jew from Brooklyn in New York City.

Because of all of this, I am excited to be witnessing the 2016 American presidential campaign and see that Bernie sanders, a man in his seventies, who had the guts and the fire to dare dream the, until he said it in May 2015, the impossible dream, that many American writers, thinkers, musicians, poets, singers, have been advocating but nobody seemed to listen. I remember vividly the year 1977 when I had the pleasure of listening to and be touched by Roberta Flack's beautiful rendering of the song "the impossible Dream" at Washington's beautiful Carter Barron open air Theatre in the uptown of 16th Street, in Northwest, DC.

https://youtu.be/H24wcLTjOBQ

How uplifting it is to consider the possibility that despite the doom and gloom of the cynics and the cruel that a new leap forward of hope and change can emerge out of the seemingly hopeless, dysfunctional, rigged, corrupt and intractable chaos of a dominant paradigm rooted in racism, militarism and greed, and wake America and the world up.

I could not let the opportunity to share how I felt pass me by. I had an opportunity to do just that with my Washington community, America and, thanks to the internet, with the world at a United States Institute of Peace (USIP) event in May 2016 examining Dr. Martin Luther King's path to peace.

You can view and hear what I said at the end of the video here:

http://www.usip.org/events/dr-martin-luther-king-s-path-peace

In America, at least on paper, freedom of thought, speech, expression, worship and organization are guaranteed by the American constitution. As someone who, like many persecuted people because of a difference of opinion, was forced to leave his country of origin due to a dominant conservative and a culture of intolerance of the powers that be to perspectives other than their own, America, in and of itself, is way ahead in this regard. It was a primary reason why I wanted to come to this country to live and to enjoy my human right to freely think, express myself and advocate for what I believe in without being persecuted.

To be able through my thoughts, words and actions live a life of purpose that has a deeper meaning and that makes sense to me; a life of purpose rooted in my dream for a new humanism whose time has come. I am glad and grateful to, finally, be able to humbly contribute my in this endeavor through the "WORD" and advocacy. I am delighted to have been among those many Americans and global citizens who have been advocating, and organizing grassroots movements for real change in both America and other parts of the world.

We all believe that humanity today desperately needs a new more moral, saner and humane politics. In a modest way, it feels wonderful that we belong to those who are doing their part to bring about a shift in public awareness, consciousness, and an awakening that can be organized democratically to impact through voting public policy that takes us away from ignorance, fear and warmongering to peacemaking and diplomacy and, hopefully, stopping the risky spiral of the dumb wars that can lead us to an imminent apocalypse. We need to renew, deepen and universalize the American dream. Because, pandering aside, it is, in essence, a human dream.

For my public support for Bernie Sander's ideas please see the below link and the Curtis Cee video interview with me at the Washington for Bernie Rally on May 23rd, 2016 at:

https://www.facebook.com/curtiscee/videos/10153501502731971/

The world needs to change. Whether in America, in Europe, in Africa or in the Middle East, the bottom-line of what I am sharing here and the lessons I learnt is that humanity has been in a perpetual quest for meaning. It has been groping for solutions through the ages and for a way forward for what each generation understood as the pursuit of its happiness. However, those efforts have oftentimes been frustrated and overwhelmed by the dominance of evil and the unleashing of man's worst demons expressed in the organized powers of racism, militarism and greed.

To counter this, humanity has been caught up in a kill or die zero sum logic and a struggle against evil. This has been articulated, with various degrees of success or failure, in ideological and political programs. While conservative and reactionary forces who control the levers of political and economic power in society continue to mobilize their forces to maintain the status quo which advantages them, progressive and revolutionary forces are in a quest to organize themselves to win by unleashing their better angels.

Through organized grassroots action they are seeking a peaceful victory of good over evil, by advocating a change agenda of social and economic justice for the working and the Middle class and doing the right thing. Socially, the Bernie Social Democratic Revolution is designed to raise peoples' awareness and consciousness and deepen their human awakening. Finally, the revolution aims at leading all the people to the liberation of the human spirit and the emergence of more enlightened 21st century humanism. This is the revolution's blueprint for birthing the transformation of the American society and making it an inspiring model of justice, peace, brotherhood, sisterhood and a beloved community rooted in the virtue of being a blessing to self, family, community and world.

http://youtu.be/cwNdWRgHa4g

Where do we go from here?

http://youtu.be/nPYkpERY6cA

As part of the DMV Bernie and our Revolution Movement in the national capital city of Washington in the District of Columbia, Virginia and Maryland, I plan to work to promote this grassroots effort in every way I know how. It starts by reforming and opening the Democratic Party at the local and the national level. I also plan to continue through this revolution to take my freedom, peace, and social, economic, environmental and racial justice advocacy to the next level.

http://www.Berniesanders.com/win

Afterword

In a few days, Donald J. Trump, the outsider, real state tycoon and inventor of the household name show "the Apprentice" and his fans who proved all the corporate media pundits and pollsters, would be sworn in as the 45th president of the world's greatest power today, the United States of America. Anger was a factor in his election.

While the American Right is celebrating a savior of white America afraid of loosing power, the American Left is bracing to save America from what they perceive as America's Benito Mussolini and America's Adolf Hitler, linked to questions about the roots causes of ideological extremism, extreme desertification, extreme poverty and violence?

So, the question becomes why are so many Americans and why are so many people everywhere angry at their politicians, governments and bureaucracies? Why are so many people so mad? Why are so many people frustrated because they feel that their governments failed to help them to be able to satisfy their basic needs for work, food, education, health and above all peace and security? Why do so many feel that the dreams they were hoping to pursue became nightmares?

That fundamentalist and extremist political rehtoric and the perceived lying of politicians from both the right and the left contributed to setting all sorts of conspiracy theories ablaze. All this was exaggerated by the ascendance of America's capitalism and the New York Wall Street and finance elitism, after the fall of the Berlin

Wall in 1989, as the be all and end all of civilization and the final defeat of Communism, the Soviet Union and of course Marxism.

The tragic events of September 11, 2001 were a passionate, albeit irrational and insane act of cruelty and hate. They revealed to us, like all other injustices and wanton violence unleashed in human history in the four corners of the world such as colonialism, apartheid, slavery and the continuous, vain and dumb wars all over the world, the level to which humans can go in barbarity and inhumanity as the relentless 24/7 television news cycle exhibit before our eyes on a daily basis.

Issues of social and economic justice have been on my mind ever since I started my life as a herder of calves in Africa at age 7. Today, at 77, I am an honorary member of President Barack Obama's Kitchen Cabinet living a few blocks from the White House in Washington, D.C. All my life I have been trying to focus on the magic and the beauty of life and of the world. Like most people today I am still wondering why is our world drifting towards a sure tragic abbys and what can we do to stop it?

There is a growing awareness and a deeper consciousness among thinkers, philosophers, scholars, believers and non believers and all those concerned and caring humans in all continents that the current nation state model which is rooted in racism, militarism and greed is the ideological root cause of our predicament which created government systems and mammoth bureaucracies that have become incompetent, corrupt and rigged in favor of the 1% rich and well connected, excluding the 99% poor, disenfranchised and marginalized and keeping them hostage. For over fifty years now many compassionate thinkers, researchers, caring intellectuals as well as many development theorists and experts at many levels, including the United Nations, have been advocating for a culture change and a paradigm shift. That, in essence, the problem is rooted in the concept and the ideas on which the status quo is founded and that this concept is now obsolete.

I liked the diagnosis 2016 presidential candidate Bernie Sanders made of the American 2008 financial meltdown as well as his prescription. Why? Because, I was a social democrat since I was 23 years old and, like him, I have always thought out of the box and believed that finding common ground and celebrating commonsense is a virtue, while all extremisms, vanity, self-righteous indulgence is repugnant, sloppy, worst demons-centered and unhealthy. The failure of the Democratic National Committee to accept the more popular and inspiring Bernie Sanders as the Democratic Party's candidate for president is a historical mistake and example of how obsolete, corrupt and rigged to the core the party bureaucracy is.

We can stop the anger and the madness as well as the fast spiral towards a sure apocalypse by being serious about really changing the culture and shifting the paradigm by thinking, saying and doing something about it everyday. There is an urgency to engage in and make this our main conversation moving forward, at the dinner table about why we need to practice honesty, better communicate and speak our truth and really care for and listen to each other's narrative. Because we all have stories and we all have narratives. Let us make the need to be heard, understood, respected, embraced and even celebrated a human right. Because narratives do matter.

What is called for today, in my view, is less vanity, greater humility, a deeper understanding and an awakening of the human spirit. The social sciences of the 21st century need to innovate and catch up with the amazing feats and advances in technology and help us have a less antagonistic, mutually exclusive and demonizing narratives to a more genuine and honest and truthful narrative of the human journey and story that can give a deeper meaning of our lives, prompt a rethinking of human civilization today.

For the world to be free, we desperately need to universalize and make the pursuit of happiness a human right for all people. To get there we need a culture and a paradigm shift for an intellectual awakening that can lead to the unleashing of the awesome power of our better angels and the liberation of our human spirit, a pre-requisite for a necessary societal transformation and the sunrise of a more peaceful, joyous and beautiful world. All will be possible if we dare to dream the big dreams starting by the dream of a quest for a New Humanism in the 21st century.

The author's story of revolution, exile and hope and his quest for freedom, justice and peace and life journey is a striving towards this goal.

Appendix

Document # 1.

My Letter to George W. Bush

Salam Sudan Foundation*
1615 L St NW Suite 340
Washington, DC 20036

[Injustice anywhere is a threat to justice everywhere].
Martin Luther King, in a letter from his Birmingham (Alabama) Jail.

***

[And ye shall know
the truth,
And the truth will make you free].
John 8:32, The Bible.

***

[Let there arise out of you
A band of people
Inviting to all that is good,

Enjoining what is right,
And forbidding what is wrong:
They are the ones
To attain felicity].
Al-imran 104, The Quran.

***

The Honorable George W. Bush
President of the United States of America
The White House, 1600 Pennsylvania Avenue

Washington, DC 20220 March 30, 2001

America's Renewal and Leadership for a World of Justice and Peace

The Honorable George W. Bush,

From a universal, inclusive, spiritual, God-centered and truth-yearning perspective, we believe that oftentimes, political Washington's cynicism, lack of an enlightened long term global vision, ignorance of and stereotyping of other cultures, haste, absence of humility and a dominant hawkish culture of violence characterized many of the previous administration's' foreign policy both in discourse (talking down to other nations) and action (gingerly showering missiles on others on the basis of questionable intelligence). We also believe that although chauvinism, narrow-mindedness, egocentrism, myopia and ignorance are the root cause of all fundamentalisms, the above American style of conducting international relations contributed, in no small measure, to perpetuating the ugly-American image and perception of this land and its good people in many parts of the world, fueling hatred and terrorism against its vital national interests worldwide. Despite its previous problems with slavery, and current problems of racism, the many errors of judgment of a number of your predecessors, and the objective limitations that are the lot of all human endeavors. The land of George Washington, Abraham Lincoln and Malcolm X, we believe, represents the world's most youthful, fascinating and inspiring ongoing experiment in democratic governance. As a unique microcosm of the whole wide world, America has the most colorful, diverse and dynamic culture as well as economy. America is also the world's number one in technology, finance, agriculture, mass media and defense.

In a world characterized by the eternal struggle between good and evil, between mediocrity and excellence and the prevalence of a culture of injustice, violence, corruption and selfishness, the land of Jefferson, despite such laws as secret evidence and racial profiling and regrettable police practices which we applaud your declaration to end, should remain a hospitable home, refuge and a haven for the persecuted. With this in mind, it became our home of choice for which we are immensely grateful and of which we are extremely proud.

The challenge of the new millennium to the America of John F. Kennedy, Martin Luther King, the Party of Lincoln and your presidency is, we believe, daring a new paradigm in international relations based on a more compassionate, inclusive, universal and enlightened dialogue of the World's diverse cultures, civilizations and religions. This is our vision for peace in the world. This is our vision for American renewal at home and American leadership for a global and humane renewal abroad. This is our American Dream.

We believe and have been advocating for the last 30 years that American ideals of liberty, democracy and human rights stand to win more by persuasion and an enlightened compassionate-leadership-by-example approach to foreign policy rather than by the globally perceived methods of coercion, cynicism, and a techno-management approach of politics as usual and superficial misleading intelligence.

To move America from the de facto Superpower that it is today, to the undisputed, respected leader of a World renewal that ought to be her mission, America, we believe, should continue the task of putting its house in order by moving seriously to fixing the many ailments bedeviling it starting by better ballot counting machines. That America can then lead by example and action not by mere rhetoric.

The nation should showcase the ideals of justice, peace, democracy, human rights and sustainable and equitable social and economic development within its own borders, which will enhance its role as the best messenger and advocate for these ideals globally. That America would be the true expression of the goodness inherent in the American people that elected you to lead America and the World at this vital milestone in humanity's history.

As you know, Mr. President, all the scriptures warn us to guard against the evil of arrogance and teach us the goodness of humility.

The day this strong and mighty America is no more perceived as arrogant but coming across as a nation of renewal, that is humble and respectful to other cultures, the sun will set on hatred, violence, war and terrorism. This is why we need to make humility an American value. Herein lies America's challenge. Herein lies America's promise to itself and to humanity. Herein lies your chance for a great legacy.

We applauded you, Mr. President, when you stated during the presidential campaign that while America must be strong, it must also be humble. As immigrants who, like the forefathers, came to this land to avoid persecution, and who cherish the spiritual and human values of our Nile Valley culture of origin, and eager to share the best of it, we believe that while arrogance is a sign of weakness humility is a sign of strength. We also believe that spirituality, faith and humility are great assets for authentic leadership. And that while the freedom of expression and religious practice in America has no parallel; our real challenge is to make humility an American virtue. What we respect about you, Mr. President, and made us confident that you have the makings of a great leader, is that, you are a man of faith and unlike many politicians you sound true, inclusive to all Faiths, and eager to lead this nation to the higher values of honor, integrity and civility enshrined in the scriptures.

This could open the way for moving America and Washington from a predominant culture of political warmongering and violence to a more humane culture of justice, compassion and peace. What better legacy for a man of faith! Finally, we wish your administration, America and the world the best under your strong yet humble, firm yet compassionate, and daring yet wise leadership.

God bless you, Mr. President, and God Bless America's and the World's renewal.

In justice and peace,
Yours respectfully,
Hashim El-Tinay

Founder and President
*[Salam Sudan Foundation is an independent, nonprofit and nonpartisan organization. It is dedicated since 1982 to advocating a universal culture of justice, peace, democracy and human rights through research, education, communication and a dialogue of cultures, civilizations and religions].

Document # 2.

Letter to Barack Obama

Obama's Legacy: Eden or Armageddon?

[Injustice anywhere is a threat to justice everywhere].
Martin Luther King Junior, in a letter from his Birmingham (Alabama) Jail.

***

[And ye shall know the truth, and the truth will make you free]
John 8:32, The Bible

***

[Let there arise out of you, A band of people, Inviting to all that is good, Enjoining what is right, And forbidding what is wrong: They are the ones to attain felicity], Al-imran 104, The Qur'an

***

[There were men who took first steps down new roads armed with nothing but their own vision] Ayn Rand

The Honorable Barack Obama
President of the United States of America
The White House,
1600 Pennsylvania Avenue Washington, DC 20220

Washington, D.C., May 5th, 2013

Subject:
A First Bold Step Toward a Beloved Community

From Kunta Kinte and Nelson Mandela to Trayvon Martin and Beyond:
Time for a New 21st century Vision for Societal Liberation and Transformation Through a Global Truth, Reconciliation, Social and Economic Justice and Peace Initiative

The Honorable Barack Obama,
Greetings of peace/salam,

Thank you for your kind letter of April 15th, 2013 and for taking the time to respond to my earlier communication and writing.

Today I am writing to you as a global citizen, a free thinker and a witness. I have been striving all my life to have a voice. Now that I do I would like to use it to give voice to the voiceless, the silent majority in the world.

I endeavor to do that by using my education to articulate their yearnings and modestly advocate for their dreams. That is why, hearing from you despite what you are enduring from Washington's dysfunctional political environment and its seemingly chronic, dominant culture of cynicism, is both humbling and reassuring.

I also write to you, Mr. President, as a free thinker first and a non-partisan, in essence, who became one because of you. As "all politics is local" I am glad to write to you as a Foggy Bottom neighbor living a few blocks from the White House. I would like you to now that I am happy that my life's journey that started at age 7 as a shepherd in Sudan's eastern Kordofan town of Um Rawaba, took me all over the world where I studied, worked and lived from Khartoum, to Lagos, to Geneva, to Dubai, to Paris, to Abu Dhabi, and finally to Washington, DC.

I am today blessed to be in a place where I am able to continue my study, research, education about American culture and politics, which has been a lifelong interest. I am delighted to be living in a community where I am able to pursue what I love, and participate in grassroots democracy. From this vantage point, while I commend your Administration's achievements so far, I at the same time honestly critique its failings. The road travelled and the list of legislations you enumerated in your letter is, despite Congress's logjam, impressive. However, the challenges that remain to be addressed are nevertheless mammoth as well as complex.

As you know Mr. President, I supported you from day one for both objective as well as subjective reasons. The objective part is based on my perspective as a diplomat, international relations and development professional, a thinker, an author with a vision for global peace, and as a peace advocate. You directly spoke to my peace vision when you declared that the war in Iraq was a "dumb war" which made me an objective ally of yours. The subjective part is based on a striking similarity of your personal and family history and story, as a hybrid, with my own.

As a researcher, I enjoyed reading all your books and specially "Dreams from My Father". I also read "Barack Obama: The Story" written by David Maraniss. They all spoke to me directly and made me an ally.

A product of a synthesis of two races, ethnicities and continents, your agenda to bring hope and change to America and the world, and your gift to articulate with brilliance and grace the legitimate yearnings of all the people, made you the dream politician and the God-sent advocate for using power as a tool to serve the common good of all, the core of my reason for being and of my vision for societal transformation and renewal in the 21st century.

I humbly but firmly believe, Mr. President, that you have a rare opportunity to take Dr. Martin Luther King's peace legacy to the next level by doing something about lessening and gradually ending the ongoing wars, as you have done so far, with the Afghan, Iraq and religious extremism wars. Intellectually, there is a need to sow the seed of ending the culture of violence by addressing the root causes of all violence. As our human experience teaches us that hate begets hate and violence begets violence, the time is ripe to consider new strategies other than the pursuit of peace by violent means. America cannot drone its way to peace.

This I believe can be done by investing in intercultural and interfaith research, education and collaboration and using innovative ideas in the social sciences and the new technologies. Judging by the horrendous and wanton violence in America and the world, the temptation to resort to brute force rather than the peaceful resolution of conflicts, and menace of the proliferation of chemical and nuclear weapons finding their way to the hands of extremists, we need to act fast.

The time for the "audacity of hope" is now, Mr. President. The time to challenge the dominant greed, selfish, fear and violence-centered paradigm is now. The time for novel ideas that can lead toward a much-needed shift in the current unhealthy culture of violence is now.

The time to save the lives of our young men and women from missions of destruction around the world, but rather train, educate and empower them to be a force for the reconstruction and the revival of our economy and society.

The time to stop sending them to fight and die in unnecessary and "dumb wars" in far away lands is now. We need to bravely acknowledge and encourage peace visions and all new thinking that can lead to a peace-centered paradigm shift of all our cultures and faith traditions, the absence of which, I believe, is in part, the root cause of violence.

Other culprits include mainstream culture's racist stereotypical perceptions that divide people. It makes it acceptable that it is ok that some of us become objects of such laws as "stand your ground". The time to end the culture that tolerates police profiling, excessive use of force, and brutality, tyranny, arrogance, self-righteousness, ignorance and victims of loss of life, poverty, disease, social and economic injustice, in now.

You know from experience, Mr. President, that politics is at its best the art of the possible. Judging by the difficulties faced by your common sense legislation on the Hill to reduce gun violence and get weapons of war off our streets, what I am saying might sound unrealistic and mere wishful thinking.

All I have is my voice. All I strive to do is to use it by giving voice to the voiceless. Because I do believe that: "it is the right thing to do". So let us do the right thing.

In peace/salam,
Dr. Hashim El-Tinay
Thinker, Writer, Peace Advocate
Foggy Bottom
Washington, DC 20037

Document # 3.

Letter to Barack Obama

[And ye shall know the truth, and the truth will make you free]. John 8:32, The Bible

***

[We have not sent you (Muhammad) but to be a mercy to the world]. The Prophets, 21: 107 The Quran

***

[Injustice anywhere is a threat to justice everywhere].

Martin Luther King, in a letter from his Birmingham (Alabama) Jail.

***

[Through the centuries there were men who took first steps down new roads armed with nothing but their own vision] Ayn Rand

***

The Honorable Barack Obama
President of the United States of America
The White House,
1600 Pennsylvania Avenue Washington, DC 20220

Washington, D.C., August 4, 2013
26 Ramadan, 1434 Hegira

Subject: Toward an Obama Legacy for Eternity:

A World of Justice and Peace: A Grassroots Peace Quest Perspective

The Honorable Barack Obama,

Greetings of peace/salam,

Thank you for your kind letter, yours and Michelle's and yours and Bill Clinton's earlier thank you notes. I consider your taking the time to respond to my writing and earlier communication as an expression of your interest to continue our electronic conversation through regular mail via your letter of April 15th, 2013. So hearing from you, despite the challenges of Washington's dysfunctional political environment and its seemingly chronic and dominant culture of cynical political posturing is both humbling and reassuring.

I see it as a testament to the virtue of a culture that respects grass roots ideas and appreciates the necessary value of listening to those who are speaking truth to power. It is proof of your qualitative listening to the people's voices and, despite the frustration caused by Republican anti Obama tactics on Capitol Hill, a bright testament to what works in American democracy. Above all it is a sign that you genuinely care to reach out and engage the larger community to access all you can of the knowledge and wisdom out there that can nourish and hopefully inform your administration's public policy.

Your Administration's achievements enumerated are, despite Congress's logjam, impressive. However, the challenges that remain to be addressed are nevertheless enormous. And believe me Mr. President, as Bill Clinton would put it: I do feel your pain! So much so that I am happy not to be in your shoes ☺! But as a democrat and a neighbor I have empathy for you and would love to see you achieve the success that we all are working for, yearning for and hoping for.

I supported you from day one, Mr. President, because, through your worldview and hope and change agenda, and your personal history as a hybrid, like me, you came close to what I consider to be an ideal and the right politician at the right time. In you I felt to have finally found a gifted advocate for my alternative peace vision.

The discovery of your ideas since your famous Boston speech at the Democratic Party Convention and your courageous anti Iraq war position, the smooth merging of our paths to serve a common cause, the arrival of Martin Luther King Junior statute to our neighborhood at the Washington National Mall next door and my monthly Foggy Bottom grassroots Peace Quest Forum in your backyard, as a neighbor (living close to the George Washington University campus, a few blocks from the White House) all inspire hope and good omen!

So please forgive me, Mr. President, if I am daydreaming. But then that is my privilege as a thinker and an author, who unlike you wields no political power, but free to imagine and dream the big dreams and share them with the universe hoping that they happen somehow! Not being a politician, I am addressing the thinker and author in you who chose politics to do something about the world.

I sense that you are genuinely driven by a desire to do your part, for the same reasons I chose advocacy. So as you made your way to the campaign trail in 2008 and went to make your case before the American people, I went to work as a volunteer for your election campaign and mobilized the community to vote and elect you as president. Division of labor of sorts!

As a humble observer of politics, I like to think of myself as a witness and a passionate peace and justice, freedom and human dignity advocate. Believe me Mr. President, I understand and know a thing or two about your frustration from the roadblocks put on your way by small politics. I have had and continue to endure persecution, prison and 40 years of exile from my country of origin, simply for having dared to have a vision, a big dream and my own voice. Simply for thinking and acting out of the box. Simply for expressing and defending my ideas.

Aware of the objective limitations of politics, the stress of managing the wide array of the Federal Government's departments and the economy, and the bubble syndrome, I am just trying to offer you a few ideas as a respite from the mammoth bureaucracy you are managing and the microscopic focus of your job. In so doing I hope to win you over, beyond the partisan bureaucracy, and engage you on an authentic, candid, meaningful, albeit sympathetic, conversation from a grassroots and civil society vintage point.

Because we the people demand that you be our Advocate-in-Chief! And to tempt you even more Mr. President, despite my age (I am 73 years young), I still have some intellectual juice in me. And yes I do have much more exciting ideas to share with you if you so wish. This is just a teaser - a tip of the iceberg!

As violence begets violence, we ought to consider new strategies that can stop the pursuit of peace by violent means. Drones and short term fixes would not do it. And frankly, instead of wasting billions of dollars, that we do not have, in unwinnable dumb wars, Mr. President, we need to lead by example and invest these billions in peace research, innovation and education from kindergarten to the grave.

You have a golden opportunity Mr. President, as a Nobel Peace Laureate to lead us into thinking out of the box and embracing ideas that can help shift this zero sum violence-death-centered paradigm that is killing us. You can harness the formidable tools at your disposal, Mr. President, to bravely imagine, invent and encourage new thinking that can lead to a peace-life-centered paradigm reset of all our cultures and faith traditions.

The UNESCO constitution of 1948 stipulates that: "since wars start in the minds of men, it is in the minds of men that the defenses of peace must be constructed". We need to lead the world by example and start by deconstructing the sham official history written by the "victors". We need to replace it by a more honest narrative and history, inclusive and respectful of all human contributions, that can be accepted by all of us and that can give legitimacy to our discourse and action.

This can lead to a better and a more balanced human awareness leading to a more genuine and much-desired human awakening. This, in my view, could be a prerequisite for taking the wind out of the sail of all extremisms opening the way for a less confrontational, politicized and divisive United Nations and world. This is how, I believe, we can contribute to a much-needed societal transformation befitting the 21st century.

The great news is that you, being the voice of progress, of those who get it, of those who are on the right side of history, you are supported by large swaths of American and world public opinions. This however is, alas and in many ways compromised by the various and ongoing challenges to your administration. They include the failure to close the controversial Guantanamo prison in Cuba, the shameful "in limbo" status of its inmates and the spectacle of their forced feeding.

Add to that the out of control drone strikes, the Benghazi tragedy, Africom, the Congo, Syria, Egypt, Palestine (I commend John Kerry's audacity to take this head on), the ongoing strife of the people in the two Sudans, Darfur, and the new Kordofan and Blue Nile tragedies (A new Sudan must be born and united because Africa Must Unite), the National Security Agency (NSA), Edward Snowden and the surveillance of our private communications and others. Despite all this, I still sincerely believe, from the perspective of my worldview, that your election in 2008 and reelection in 2012 reflected a high point in the evolution and maturing of American democracy.

I also believe that from a spiritual perspective, your arrival on the political landscape is a blessing to America and the world, whence my ambition for you to deliver on the big dreams for both. My ambition for you and that of millions of hybrids of the world, like us, and other forward looking people, is for you to, as you often say to really "seize the moment".

Instead of conducting international relations, like George W. Bush, by reaction and military force, we want you to avoid the trap of being dragged, despite your arguments, into, what might turn out to be yet another "dumb war". We want you to take the moral high ground on Syria by bringing all the protagonists to the negotiating table; help them learn to dialogue, seek common ground and arrive at a politically negotiated settlement. This is how you can make your mark and wrench a legacy of a World of Justice and Peace, which we the people, and the whole world expect of you. We want you to take, in so doing, Martin Luther King's legacy to the next level and make this an Obama and the progressive peoples' legacy for eternity. Now that is leading from the front, Mr. President.

This will be your best response to the Republicans and all those who are caught up in a trigger-happy mode and who chose to be on the wrong side of history. This will be your best response to those who accepted to remain hostage to and barricaded on their self-righteous and self-centered supremacist and racist worldview. This will be your best response to all those refusing to open their eyes and see the bigger picture. A legacy that can liberate and take us all to the mountaintop so that we can at long last, and finally, be set free, and get to the Promised Land.

And you know very well, Mr. President, the impact of the social media in this day and age and that public opinion that supports you does rule the world. Your talents as a community organizer in Chicago, and your building Organizing for America (OFA) and Organizing for Action (OFA), the best grassroots political organizations the world has ever known are great assets. In addition, you also have the education, the knowledge, the authenticity, your presidential experience, amazing gifts and an evolving worldview to realize the Dream.

Beyond America you have an African and indeed a global constituency. You represent both the chasm in our broken human family as well as the promise of its reunion that a global process of truth and reconciliation through a creative synthesis could bring about. Will you, Mr. President?

Finally, this last question Mr. President, if not you, who? And if not now, when? Really! Honestly!

Will you seize the moment? I certainly hope so and so are the billions of people you inspired across the world by your eloquence, humility and grace.

Wishing you a happy birthday, Mr. President!

Let us continue.

Respectfully,

In peace/salam
Your neighbor,

Dr. Hashim El-Tinay
Thinker, Author, Peace Advocate
Foggy Bottom
Washington, DC 20037 -2508

Document # 4

Saint Mary's Court

My Election Victory Speech

A Vision for Change June 2014

Hashim El-Tinay,

"Give me a place to stand on, and I shall
transform myself and change the world"

Gratitude:

It is said that the happiest people in the world do not have the best of everything; they just make the best of everything. This applies to all of us.

In dynamic and free societies all institutions are challenged to prove their relevance. Today universities are struggling because of the shift to online education, and every institution has to retool itself in order to be relevant. We have to continue to prove our relevance and to meet people where they are.

In his famous November 2008 election Chicago thank you speech president Obama said that the American citizens and voters clearly confirmed that by electing him, a son of an African father and a Caucasian mother, all was possible in America, if you worked for it.

By the same token, if a black man like me, with a name like mine, coming from an African and Arab country like mine, a country that even the state department had a problem classifying until it was split into two in July 2011; and someone who became an American citizen in 2002 competing with two American born citizens, can be elected by you as president of an association of a community sitting at the epicenter of Washington, DC, then truly all is possible in America.

So I am grateful for all those who voted for me and gave me their trust and goodwill and embraced of my change agenda by and elected me to serve as your president for the next two years. I suppose those of them who knew that in 2010 I declared running for president of Sudan decided to make me president here now that the Sudan I wanted to be president of is, because of small politics, alas, no more!

Second, thanks for the outgoing president Madame Bernice Chucku and Philip Schrefer, president of the nominations committee and their teams and all the volunteers who made all this possible.

Third, thanks for SMC Board, Management and staff under Margaret Pully's and Mr. Khan's leadership and their teams. Fourth, thanks to the Foggy Bottom- FRIENDS- George Washington University (GWU), and the larger Washington, DC communities that, since 1996, helped me reclaim my voice, refine my vision and find a place to stand on among all of you.

Finally, thanks for the moral and material support and the understanding and solidarity of my family and many friends in America, the Sudan and around the world.

Vision and Direction:

Contribute to the development of the SMC community experiment by helping people fulfill their dreams and making it a beloved community, a sanctuary of peace and compassion where its residents can pursue happiness through focusing on their Wellness, Wisdom and Well being (my 3 W's). (Please sign up on one of the three Ws and make a difference)

Mission:

Realize this vision by changing the narrative, the culture, the focus, the conversation and the mindset and seeking everybody's embrace of a more positive disposition rooted in mutual goodwill, trust and respect. Open opportunities for people to connect one-on-one or in small circles thus liberating our human spirit, and unleashing your untapped creative human potential and start to better enjoy every day as a gift by focusing on our Wellness, Wisdom and Well Being (my 3 W's). (Please sign up and join one of the three Ws and make a difference)

Tools:

Our new team's work will be guided by a respectful, thoughtful, transparent, truthful, compassionate and firm Servant-leadership focus. We expect no less from each one of you, from the SMC management and board. We will act as facilitators to best grasp and advocate for your ideas, and satisfy your needs and aspirations. We intend to fix the serious communication deficit among many of us that is keeping us separate, divided and unequal. We intend to work collaboratively and liaise efficiently with the SMC management and board and arrive at a satisfactory resolution of the seemingly unreachable goal of the mandatory food program puzzle and the many other issues of discord, once and for all.

This is how I envisage my role and that of our new team to serve you in the coming two years. But we cannot do it without your help and input, as you are our most precious resource. In addition to signing up and joining the new proposed circles/groups, our channels of communication will be open to your constructive ideas and suggestions. A simple and a most convenient way to share with us and do your part is to drop us a note in the association's suggestions' box, available for you 24/7 in the library.

Our premise is that each and every one of you is a leader on his or her own right. Our obligation to you is to help channel and systematize your positive energy as facilitators for greater clarity, unity in diversity, and greater harmony. This is how we can work together with all of you to improve the socio-economic, cultural and spiritual quality of our lives.

As many of you know and as I said in my campaign statement I come to this with an open heart, mind and spirit. I am grateful that you gave me this wonderful, albeit challenging opportunity to meaningfully connect and learn from each one of you.

Our greatest asset resides in you, our members and your embrace of this vision. I will bring my diplomatic, cross-cultural and interfaith communication experience and my long pursuit of conflict resolution and work for more peaceful communities and world to the task. I trust that we can, together, through genuine collaborative dialogue; better understanding and hard work transform the spirit of this place, solve problems and add more joy, fun and happiness to our lives.

While appreciative and grateful for your trust and to lead the association with a mandate to bring about desired change, we will build on all that is positive that we inherited from the hard work done towards the pursuit of our common happiness.

As your new president, our new team, and I intend to lead by listening and engaging with you and SMC board and management to find real solutions to real problems so that together we can make a qualitative difference in our collective Wellness, Wisdom and Wellbeing, by focusing on them as follows:

1) Create an atmosphere of trust, goodwill, respect and wellness between all of us based on a voluntary, substantive social grouping plan and resolve the lingering issues of contention like the mandatory food program, and round the sharp edges

in the rare cases of out-of-control unacceptable attitudes and behaviors by a few who disturb our peace.

(Please sign up for new activities options and make a difference).

2) Create an atmosphere of trust, goodwill, respect and wisdom between the residents and the SMC management to move from a polarized culture of zero sum confrontation and what some perceive as a rigid enforcement by management to a more considerate and thoughtful culture of justice and compassionate service. With excellent communication, transparency, accountability, thoughtful dialogue and truth we can all learn, grow, improve, find solutions to problems and be happier and wiser for it. (Please sign up for new activities options and make a difference)

3) Create an atmosphere of trust, goodwill, respect and well being by establishing a reliable who's-who database for the residents, SMC board and management as a vital source of knowledge that can better inform and nourish our knowing one another better. This could provide us with more transparency and equity. (Please sign up for new activities options and make a difference).

As our human capital, the database can become a valuable resource of expertise and wisdom and give face and meaning to our community members. A few perceive SMC at best as no more than a faceless comfortable inn and at worst as a clean warehouse of bodies of some lucky Washington's seniors. (Please sign up for new activities options and make a difference)

Because "in the beginning was the word", my monthly Peace Quest Forum since 2010 has been a call to engage in a meaningful conversation and an invitation on how to reach common ground and build a beloved community of caring friends. I am grateful for those who answered the call.

Standing on SMC let us start anew. Let us make the dining area a happier venue and a place to look forward to go to because we will have a good time, meet new good and interesting people, have fun and enjoy a healthy meal. It can become a "happy hour" fun place of sorts that is more about fellowship than just about food.

At this stage of our lives, we all know how precious time is and especially for those of us striving to make the best of their golden years. As a free people we are blessed to have various options and different lifestyles to pursue our happiness. There should, however, be room for those who want to give back at SMC and this is where the SMCRA must innovate and lead.

The good news is that every day is the first day of the rest of our lives. How beautiful it would be to appreciate it as a wondrous gift to be lived fully! A new opportunity to renew, find deeper meaning and adopt a more positive and appreciative attitude to life. It would be great if we could all listen more, share meaningfully more, focus on positive conversations more, open ourselves more, reach out more, seek friendship more, enjoy humor, fun, and beauty to renew and deepen the dream and give thanks.

All what I am trying to say is that my vision for change is all about your wellness, wisdom and wellbeing. Let us seize this incredible opportunity and make the best of it by embracing change. Can you help us become better organized so that we can together, during the coming two years, start writing a new chapter in the book of our common journey of transformation and change? Can we make our tomorrows better than our yesterdays by changing our present?

How can we address poverty in our midst and identify and find new resources to help those of us who need help? How can we start conversations around issues of common concern to all of us and use that as an opportunity to engage with one another? Could this be a way to make our humble contribution to the ongoing conversations around dining tables around the globe about the rich and the poor, the over class and the underclass, the 1% and the 99%? What should the new American dream look like? How can we find solutions to our problems and how Germany beat Brazil so bad at the World Cup?

Because life is short standing on this vision and SMC and focused on our wellness, wisdom and wellbeing, we are privileged to be able to add humor to the mix and not take ourselves too seriously. I happened to believe that we might be able to enhance our wellbeing by being philosophical, humble, kind, gracious, and a blessing and a mercy to one another. I also happened to believe that we might be able to enhance our wellbeing by liberating our human spirit, build a beloved community, and lead by example.

Since all politics is local and is becoming more and more global, I happened to believe that we might be able to enhance our wellbeing by effecting change here and proceed to really change the world for the better, one person at a time, one community at a time, one city at a time and one country at a time.

Finally, I happened to believe that we might be able to enhance our wellbeing by being audacious, daring to dream the big dreams, and with the help of the "Merciful and the Compassionate", realize them so that we can all reach the "Promised Land". I know I am ready. I know that some of you are too? Let us go to work and have some fun too!

Thank you.

Document # 5

Recommended Reading:

1 - Nelson Mandela:
Long Walk to Freedom: The Autobiography of Nelson Mandela

2 - Amilcar Cabral
Revolutionary Leadership And People's War

3 - Martin Luther King, Junior
The Autobiography of Martin Luther King, Jr.

4 - Barack Hussein Obama:
   a) The Audacity of Hope:
       Thoughts on Reclaiming the American Dream

   b) Dreams from My Father:
       A Story of Race and Inheritance

   c) Change We Can Believe In:
       Barack Obama's Plan to Renew America's Promise

5 - Michelle Obama in her Own Words:
The Views and Values of America's First Lady

6 - Pierre Orelus
Race, Power, and the Obama Legacy

7 - Thomas Frank Interviews Cornel West

8 - Noam Chomsky:
Profit Over People: Neoliberalism & Global Order

9 - CORNEL WEST

10 - Ryan Holiday
Ego is the Enemy

11 - AbdelKarim AlKabli:
Melodies Not Militants,
An African Artist's Message of Hope, 2015

12 - Mansour Khalid:
    a)   The Paradox of the Two Sudans, 2015

    b)   War and Peace in the Sudan

13 - Francis Deng
Bound By Conflict, Dilemmas of the Two Sudans

14 - Alan Moorehead:
The Blue Nile

15 - Alan Moorehead:
The White Nile,

16 - Winston Churchill,
The River War

17 - Ghana: The Autobiography of Kwame Nkrumah

18 - Sulayman Nyang
Islam in the United States of America

19 - Ali Mazrui
The Politics of War and the Culture of Violence: North South Essays

20 - Edward Said
Culture and Imperialism

21 - Dinesh D'Souza
What's So Great About America

22 - Jonathan Spence
Mao Zedong: A Life

23 - Montesquieu:
The Spirit of the Laws (Cambridge Texts in the History of Political Thought)

24 - Jon Meacham
Thomas Jefferson: The Art of Power

25 - Jonathan Tasini
The Essential Bernie Sanders and His Vision for America

26 - Samuel Huntington,
The Clash of Civilizations and the Making of the New World Order

27 - Kwame Nkrumah
The Autobiography of Kwame Nkrumah

28 - Enrique Dussel
Philosophy of Liberation

29 - Samir Amin
    1 - From Capitalism to Civilization
    2 - Empire of Chaos

30 - Hashim El-Tinay
Nile Sunrise:
Winds of Revolution and Liberation in Africa & the Middle East, the
Case of Sudan

Biography

Dr. Hashim El- Tinay
Peace Advocate,
Founder/President

The International Peace Quest Institute (IPQI)

As founder and president of the International Peace Quest Institute (IPQI), a think tank/civil society organization/NGO created in Paris in 1985 and since 1998 operating out of Washington, DC with representatives in Paris and Nairobi and since June 2006 in Khartoum. Dr. El-Tinay contributed, and quietly, through his persistent advocacy for a more freedom, social, economic, racial and environmental justice as a way to a peaceful and humane world, to a call for societal transformation in the 21st century and the shift in American culture toward a peace rather than a war-centered culture locally, regionally and globally.

After the signing of the Sudan Comprehensive Peace Agreement (CPA) on January 9th, 2005 in Nairobi, IPQI organized a number of workshops and forums in Washington, DC to explain to the media, the American public and all those following Sudanese developments the CPA's significance to both American and Sudanese national interest, the future of Sudanese-American relations and its promise for moving the world toward a culture of peace. These included think tanks, research institutes, universities, corporations, and faith and community leaders.

Dr. Hashim El-Tinay, is a Sudanese-American researcher, published author, public speaker, writer, and an international cross-cultural, interfaith relations and language consultant. He has been a passionate advocate for justice, peace, democracy and human rights and dignity, locally and globally, since his university days, and has been working tirelessly since 1985 for peace and justice through cross-cultural and interfaith cooperation. As a Muslim peace advocate Hashim has been explaining Islam from an Abrahamic perspective, as the last Divine message of universal mercy, justice, peace and human dignity.

In recognition of his dedication to peace and human rights, Dr. El-Tinay is the recipient of several **Peacemaker in Action and Ambassador of Peace Awards**. Dr. El-Tinay has been involved with faith-based and secular educational institutions to consider cross-cultural and interfaith strategies for global justice, peace, democracy, human rights and dignity and sustainable social and economic development. Dr. El-Tinay has been sharing his universal vision worldwide through public speaking and writing in Arabic, English and French highlighting a unique perspective rooted in the Sudanese, Afro-Arab, and Nile Valley 5,000 year spiritual heritage.

He believes that working through grassroots and people-to-people education and public diplomacy for a better understanding between religions, cultures and civilizations is the best way to serve the cause of world peace and the renewal of World civilization. He has been quietly working through deeper cultural and spiritual awareness between people to bridging the gap of understanding between America, Europe and the Muslim world and, beyond politics, to improving relations between the American and Sudanese peoples.

He is also an assembly member-at-large of the Interfaith Conference of Metropolitan Washington (IFC), an active member of the Woodstock Center's Inter-religious Dialogue on Education, Georgetown University and a member of the board of the National Campaign for a Peace Tax Fund (NCPTF).

Before settling in Washington, DC in 1998, Dr. El-Tinay resided for 20 years, in Paris, France, where he founded in 1985 the International Peace Quest Institute (IPQI)/ Salam Sudan Foundation (SSF), an international think tank/NGO promoting the emergence of a culture of peace.

Moreover, he established and was editor-in-chief of SSF's community publication Le Messager (The Peace Quest Messenger), whose originality resided in providing a forum for an open and calm debate on religion, spirituality, the West and issues of justice, international development, from a universal, inclusive perspective. He created El-Tinay & Associates, an international cross-cultural relations and language consultancy firm, now based in Washington, DC.

In 1986 and as a result of the Sudanese people's ouster of the second military dictatorship [1969-1985], though non-partisan, El-Tinay heeded the call of his hometown grassroots community in Um Ruwaba, in the Sudanese Midwest and ran for a seat in Parliament. After a close but unsuccessful race (an outcome that later proved to be a blessing) he returned to continue his professional and advocacy work in Paris.

Prior to that Dr. El-Tinay worked as a Liaison Officer in the International Cooperation and External Relations Department of the United Nations Educational, Scientific and Cultural Organization (UNESCO) in Paris and as a consultant with the Philosophy Division of the Social Sciences Sector of UNESCO. He left UNESCO to pursue a doctoral research in international relations at the University of the Sorbonne, writing, public speaking and advocacy.

His brilliant and dynamic career started in 1965 serving for ten years as a Sudanese diplomat in Khartoum, Sudan, Paris, France and Lagos, Nigeria. For ideological differences, El-Tinay resigned, chose to emigrate and became Associate Secretary of World University Service [WUS], an international NGO, in Geneva, Switzerland, that contributed to the struggle against colonialism in Africa and apartheid in South Africa and supported the education of Palestinian refugee students. El-Tinay also worked as a Public Affairs Specialist at the Information and Public Affairs Department of the World Bank in Washington, D.C. He resigned from the World Bank, to pursue his quest for a more just and meaningful calling through research, writing, public speaking and advocacy.

El-Tinay, a believer in continuous education, has a bachelor of law degree from Khartoum University (1965), a Masters in diplomacy and international relations from the International Institute of Public Administration/Sorbonne in Paris (1968) and a Doctorate summa Cum Laude with greatest distinction in international relations from Strassford University in the United Kingdom in 2003.